Come Back, Little Sheba

by WILLIAM INGE

Random House  *New York*

Frontispiece Photograph by Vandamm

Come Back, Little Sheba was originally produced September 12, 1949, at the Westport Country Playhouse, Westport, Connecticut.

PRINTED IN THE UNITED STATES
AT THE COUNTRY LIFE PRESS, GARDEN CITY, N.Y.

For
PHYLLIS ANDERSON

COME BACK, LITTLE SHEBA *was first presented by The Theatre Guild at the Booth Theatre, New York City, on February 15, 1950, with the following cast:*

(IN ORDER OF APPEARANCE)

DOC	Sidney Blackmer
MARIE	Joan Lorring
LOLA	Shirley Booth
TURK	Lonny Chapman
POSTMAN	Daniel Reed
MRS. COFFMAN	Olga Fabian
MILKMAN	John Randolph
MESSENGER	Arnold Schulman
BRUCE	Robert Cunningham
ED ANDERSON	Wilson Brooks
ELMO HUSTON	Paul Krauss

Directed by Daniel Mann

Setting and lighting designed by Howard Bay

Costumes by Lucille Little

Production under the supervision of Lawrence Langner and Theresa Helburn

Associate Producer, Phyllis Anderson

SCENE

An old house in a run-down neighborhood of a Midwestern city.

ACT ONE

Scene I. Morning in late spring.
Scene II. The same evening, after supper.

ACT TWO

Scene I. The following morning.
Scene II. Late afternoon the same day.
Scene III. 5:30 the next morning.
Scene IV. Morning, a week later.

ACT ONE

ACT ONE

Scene I

The stage is empty.

It is the downstairs of an old house in one of those semi-respectable neighborhoods in a Midwestern city. The stage is divided into two rooms, the living room at right and the kitchen at left, with a stairway and a door between. At the foot of the stairway is a small table with a telephone on it. The time is about 8:00 A.M., a morning in the late spring.

At rise of curtain the sun hasn't come out in full force and outside the atmosphere is a little gray. The house is extremely cluttered and even dirty. The living room somehow manages to convey the atmosphere of the twenties, decorated with cheap pretense at niceness and respectability. The general effect is one of fussy awkwardness. The furniture is all heavy and rounded-looking, the chairs and davenport being covered with a shiny mohair. The davenport is littered and there are lace antimacassars on all the chairs. In such areas, houses are so close together, they hide each other from the sunlight. What sun could come through the window, at right, is dimmed by the smoky glass curtains. In the kitchen there is a table, center. On it are piled dirty dishes from supper the night before. Woodwork in the kitchen is dark and grimy. No industry whatsoever has been spent in making it one of those white, cheerful rooms that we commonly think kitchens should be. There is no action on stage for several seconds.

DOC *comes downstairs to kitchen. His coat is on back of chair, center. He straightens chair, takes roll from bag on drainboard, folds bag and tucks it behind sink. He lights stove*

3

and goes to table, fills dishpan there and takes it to sink. Turns on water, tucks towel in vest for apron. He goes to chair and says prayer. Then he crosses to stove, takes frying pan to sink and turns on water.

MARIE, *a young girl of eighteen or nineteen who rooms in the house, comes out of her bedroom (next to the living room), skipping airily into the kitchen. Her hair is piled in curls on top of her head and she wears a sheer dainty negligee and smart, feathery mules on her feet. She has the cheerfulness only youth can feel in the morning.*

MARIE
(Goes to chair, opens pocketbook there)
Hi!

DOC
Well, well, how is our star boarder this morning?

MARIE
Fine.

DOC
Want your breakfast now?

MARIE
Just my fruit juice. I'll drink it while I dress and have my breakfast later.

DOC
(Places two glasses on table)
Up a little early, aren't you?

MARIE
I have to get to the library and check out some books before anyone else gets them.

DOC
Yes, you want to study hard, Marie, learn to be a fine artist some day. Paint lots of beautiful pictures. I remember a pic-

ture my mother had over the mantelpiece at home, a picture
of a cathedral in a sunset, one of those big cathedrals in
Europe somewhere. Made you feel religious just to look at it.

MARIE

These books aren't for art, they're for biology. I have an
exam.

DOC

Biology? Why do they make you take biology?

MARIE
(*Laughs*)
It's required. Didn't you have to take biology when you
were in college?

DOC

Well . . . yes, but I was preparing to study medicine, so
of course I *had* to take biology and things like that. You see—
I was going to be a real doctor then—only I left college my
third year.

MARIE

What's the matter? Didn't you like the pre-med course?

DOC

Yes, of course . . . I had to give it up.

MARIE

Why?

DOC
(*Goes to stove with roll on plate—evasive*)
I'll put your sweet roll in now, Marie, so it will be nice and
warm for you when you want it.

MARIE

Dr. Delaney, you're so nice to your wife, and you're so nice
to me, as a matter of fact, you're so nice to everyone. I hope

my husband is as nice as you are. Most husbands would never think of getting their own breakfast.

DOC
(*Very pleased with this*)
... uh ... you might as well sit down now and ... yes, sit here and I'll serve you your breakfast now, Marie, and we can eat it together, the two of us.

MARIE
(*A light little laugh as she starts dancing away from him*)
No, I like to bathe first and feel that I'm all fresh and clean to start the day. I'm going to hop into the tub now. See you later. (*She goes upstairs.*)

DOC
(*The words appeal to him*)
Yes, fresh and clean—
(DOC *shows disappointment but goes on in businesslike way setting his breakfast on the table.*)

MARIE
(*Offstage*)
Mrs. Delaney.

LOLA
(*Offstage*)
'Mornin', honey.
(*Then* LOLA *comes downstairs. She is a contrast to* DOC's *neat cleanliness, and* MARIE's. *Over a nightdress she wears a lumpy kimono. Her eyes are dim with a morning expression of disillusionment, as though she had had a beautiful dream during the night and found on waking none of it was true. On her feet are worn dirty comfies.*)

LOLA
(*With some self-pity*)
I can't sleep late like I used to. It used to be I could sleep

till noon if I wanted to, but I can't any more. I don't know why.

DOC

Habits change. Here's your fruit juice.

LOLA
(*Taking it*)

I oughta be gettin' your breakfast, Doc, instead of you gettin' mine.

DOC

I have to get up anyway, Baby.

LOLA
(*Sadly*)

I had another dream last night.

DOC
(*Pours coffee*)

About Little Sheba?

LOLA
(*With sudden animation*)

It was just as real. I dreamt I put her on a leash and we walked downtown—to do some shopping. All the people on the street turned around to admire her, and I felt so proud. Then we started to walk, and the blocks started going by so fast that Little Sheba couldn't keep up with me. Suddenly, I looked around and Little Sheba was gone. Isn't that funny? I looked everywhere for her but I couldn't find her. And I stood there feeling sort of afraid. (*Pause*) Do you suppose that means anything?

DOC

Dreams are funny.

LOLA

Do you suppose it means Little Sheba is going to come back?

DOC

I don't know, Baby.

LOLA

(*Petulant*)

I miss her so, Doc. She was such a cute little puppy. Wasn't she cute?

DOC

(*Smiles with the reminiscence*)

Yes, she was cute.

LOLA

Remember how white and fluffy she used to be after I gave her a bath? And how her little hind-end wagged from side to side when she walked?

DOC

(*An appealing memory*)

I remember.

LOLA

She was such a cute little puppy. I hated to see her grow old, didn't you, Doc?

DOC

Yah. Little Sheba should have stayed young forever. Some things should never grow old. That's what it amounts to, I guess.

LOLA

She's been gone for such a long time. What do you suppose ever happened to her?

DOC

You can't ever tell.

LOLA

(*With anxiety*)

Do you suppose she got run over by a car? Or do you think that old Mrs. Coffman next door poisoned her? I wouldn't be a bit surprised.

DOC

No, Baby. She just disappeared. That's all we know.

LOLA

(*Redundantly*)

Just vanished one day . . . vanished into thin air.
  (*As though in a dream.*)

DOC

I told you I'd find you another one, Baby.

LOLA

(*Pessimistically*)

You couldn't ever find another puppy as cute as Little
Sheba.

DOC

(*Back to reality*)

Want an egg?

LOLA

No. Just this coffee. (*He pours coffee and sits down to breakfast.* LOLA, *suddenly*) Have you said your prayer, Doc?

DOC

Yes, Baby.

LOLA

And did you ask God to be with you—all through the day,
and keep you strong?

DOC

Yes, Baby.

LOLA

Then God will be with you, Docky. He's been with you
almost a year now and I'm so proud of you.

DOC

(*Preening a little*)

Sometimes I feel sorta proud of myself.

LOLA

Say your prayer, Doc. I like to hear it.

DOC

(*Matter-of-factly*)

God grant me the serenity to accept the things I cannot change, courage to change the things I can, and wisdom always to tell the difference. *AA Reinhold Niebuhr* *know*

LOLA

That's nice. That's so pretty. When I think of the way you used to drink, always getting into fights, we had so much trouble. I was so scared! I never knew what was going to happen.

DOC

That was a long time ago, Baby.

LOLA

I know it, Daddy. I know how you're going to be when you come home now.

(*She kisses him lightly.*)

DOC

I don't know what I would have done without you.

LOLA

And now you've been sober almost a year.

DOC

Yep. A year next month.

(*He rises and goes to the sink with coffee cup and two glasses, rinsing them.*)

LOLA

Do you have to go to the meeting tonight?

DOC

No. I can skip the meetings now for a while.

LOLA

Oh, good! Then you can take me to a movie.

DOC

Sorry, Baby. I'm going out on some Twelfth Step work with Ed Anderson.

LOLA

What's that?

DOC
(*Drying the glasses*)

I showed you that list of twelve steps the Alcoholics Anonymous have to follow. This is the final one. After you learn to stay dry yourself, then you go out and help other guys that need it.

LOLA

Oh!

DOC
(*Goes to sink*)

When we help others, we help ourselves.

LOLA

I know what you mean. Whenever I help Marie in some way, it makes me feel good.

DOC

Yah.
(LOLA *takes her cup to* DOC *and he washes it.*)
Yes, but this is a lot different, Baby. When I go out to help some poor drunk, I have to give him courage—to stay sober like I've stayed sober. Most alcoholics are disappointed men ... They need courage ...

LOLA

You weren't ever disappointed, were you, Daddy?

DOC

(*After another evasive pause*)

The important thing is to forget the past and live for the present. And stay sober doing it.

LOLA

Who do you have to help tonight?

DOC

Some guy they picked up on Skid Row last night. (*Gets his coat from back of chair*) They got him at the City Hospital. I kinda dread it.

LOLA

I thought you said it helped you.

DOC

(*Puts on coat*)

It does, if you can stand it. I did some Twelfth Step work down there once before. They put alcoholics right in with the crazy people. It's horrible—these men all twisted and shaking—eyes all foggy and full of pain. Some guy there with his fists clamped together, so he couldn't kill anyone. There was a young man, just a *young* man, had scratched his eyes out.

LOLA

(*Cringing*)

Don't, Daddy. Seems a shame to take a man there just 'cause he got drunk.

DOC

Well, they'll sober a man up. That's the important thing. Let's not talk about it any more.

LOLA

(*With relief*)

Rita Hayworth's on tonight, out at the Plaza. Don't you want to see it?

DOC

Maybe Marie will go with you.

LOLA

Oh, no. She's probably going out with Turk tonight.

DOC

She's too nice a girl to be going out with a guy like Turk.

LOLA

I don't know why, Daddy. Turk's nice. (*Cuts coffee cake.*)

DOC

A guy like that doesn't have any respect for *nice* young girls. You can tell that by looking at him.

LOLA

I never saw Marie object to any of the love-making.

DOC

A big, brawny bozo like Turk, he probably forces her to kiss him.

LOLA

Daddy, that's not so at all. I came in the back way once when they were in the living room, and she was kissing him like he was Rudolph Valentino.

DOC

(*An angry denial*)

Marie is a nice girl.

LOLA

I know she's nice. I just said she and Turk were doing some tall spooning. It wouldn't surprise me any if . . .

DOC

Honey, I don't want to hear any more about it.

LOLA

You try to make out like every young girl is Jennifer Jones in the *Song of Bernadette*.

DOC

I do not. I just like to believe that young people like her are clean and decent. . . .
(MARIE *comes downstairs.*)

MARIE

Hi!
(*Gets cup and saucer from drainboard.*)

LOLA
(*At stove*)

There's an extra sweet roll for you this morning, honey. I didn't want mine.

MARIE

One's plenty, thank you.

DOC

How soon do you leave this morning?
(LOLA *brings coffee.*)

MARIE
(*Eating*)

As soon as I finish my breakfast.

DOC

Well, I'll wait and we can walk to the corner together.

MARIE

Oh, I'm sorry, Doc. Turk's coming by. He has to go to the library, too.

DOC

Oh, well, I'm not going to be competition with a football player. (*To* LOLA) It's a nice spring morning. Wanta walk to the office with me?

LOLA

I look too terrible, Daddy. I ain't even dressed.

DOC

Kiss Daddy good-bye.

LOLA

(*Gets up and kisses him softly*)

Bye, bye, Daddy. If you get hungry, come home and I'll have something for you.

MARIE

(*Joking*)

Aren't you going to kiss *me*, Dr. Delaney?

(LOLA *eggs* DOC *to go ahead.*)

DOC

(*Startled, hesitates, forces himself to realize she is only joking and manages to answer*)

Can't spend my time kissing *all* the girls.

(MARIE *laughs.* DOC *goes into living room while* LOLA *and* MARIE *continue talking.* MARIE's *scarf is tossed over his hat on chair, so he picks it up, then looks at it fondly, holding it in the air inspecting its delicate gracefulness. He drops it back on chair and goes out.*)

MARIE

I think Dr. Delaney is so nice.

LOLA

(*She is by the closet now, where she keeps a few personal articles. She is getting into a more becoming smock*)

When did you say Turk was coming by?

MARIE

Said he'd be here about 9:30. (DOC *exits, hearing the line about* TURK) That's a pretty smock.

LOLA

(*Goes to table, sits in chair and changes shoes*)
It'll be better to work around the house in.

MARIE

(*Not sounding exactly cheerful*)
Mrs. Delaney, I'm expecting a telegram this morning. Would you leave it on my dresser for me when it comes?

LOLA

Sure, honey. No bad news, I hope.

MARIE

Oh, no! It's from Bruce.

LOLA

(MARIE's *boy friends are one of her liveliest interests*)
Oh, your boy friend in Cincinnati. Is he coming to see you?

MARIE

I guess so.

LOLA

I'm just dying to meet him.

MARIE

(*Changing the subject*)
Really, Mrs. Delaney, you and Doc have been so nice to me. I just want you to know I appreciate it.

LOLA

Thanks, honey.

MARIE

You've been like a father and mother to me. I appreciate it.

LOLA

Thanks, honey.

MARIE

Turk was saying just the other night what good sports you both are.

LOLA

(*Brushing hair*)

That so?

MARIE

Honest. He said it was just as much fun being with you as with kids our own age.

LOLA

(*Couldn't be more flattered*)

Oh, I like that Turk. He reminds me of a boy I used to know in high school, Dutch McCoy. Where did you ever meet him?

MARIE

In art class.

LOLA

Turk take art?

MARIE

(*Laughs*)

No. It was in a life class. He was modeling. Lots of the athletes do that. It pays them a dollar an hour.

LOLA

That's nice.

MARIE

Mrs. Delaney? I've got some corrections to make in some of my drawings. Is it all right if I bring Turk home this morning to pose for me? It'll just take a few minutes.

LOLA

Sure, honey.

MARIE

There's a contest on now. They're giving a prize for the best drawing to use for advertising the Spring Relays.

LOLA

And you're going to do a picture of Turk? That's nice. (*A sudden thought*) Doc's gonna be gone tonight. You and Turk can have the living room if you want to. (*A little secretively.*)

MARIE

(*This is a temptation*)

O.K. Thanks.

(*Exits to bedroom.*)

LOLA

Tell me more about Bruce.

(*Follows her to bedroom door.*)

MARIE

(*Offstage in bedroom. Remembering her affinity*)

Well, he comes from one of the best families in Cincinnati. And they have a great big house. And they have a maid, too. And he's got a wonderful personality. He makes $300 a month.

LOLA

That so?

MARIE

And he stays at the best hotels. His company insists on it. (*Enters.*)

LOLA

Do you like him as well as Turk?

(*Buttoning up back af* MARIE's *blouse.*)

MARIE

(*Evasive*)

Bruce is so dependable, and . . . he's a gentleman, too.

LOLA

Are you goin' to marry him, honey?

MARIE

Maybe, after I graduate from college and he feels he can support a wife and children. I'm going to have lots and lots of children.

LOLA

I wanted children, too. When I lost my baby and found out I couldn't have any more, I didn't know what to do with myself. I wanted to get a job, but Doc wouldn't hear of it.

MARIE

Bruce is going to come into a lot of money some day. His uncle made a fortune in men's garters. (*Exits into her room.*)

LOLA

(*Leaning on door frame*)

Doc was a rich boy when I married him. His mother left him $25,000 when she died. (*Disillusioned*) It took him a lot to get his office started and everything . . . then, he got sick. (*She makes a futile gesture; then on the bright side*) But Doc's always good to me . . . *now.*

MARIE

(*Re-enters*)

Oh, Doc's a peach.

LOLA

I used to be pretty, something like you. (*She gets her picture from table*) I was Beauty Queen of the senior class in high school. My dad was awful strict, though. Once he caught me holding hands with that good-looking Dutch McCoy. Dad sent Dutch home, and wouldn't let me go out after supper for a whole month. Daddy would never let me go out with boys much. Just because I was pretty. He was afraid all

the boys would get the wrong idea—*you* know. I never had
any fun at all until I met Doc.

MARIE

Sometimes I'm glad I didn't know my father. Mom always
let me do pretty much as I please.

LOLA

Doc was the first boy my dad ever let me go out with. We
got married that sping.
>   (*Replaces picture.* MARIE *sits on couch, puts on shoes
>   and socks.*)

MARIE

What did your father think of that?

LOLA

We came right to the city then. And, well, Doc gave up his
pre-med course and went to Chiropractor School instead.

MARIE

You must have been married awful young.

LOLA

Oh, yes. Eighteen.

MARIE

That must have made your father really mad.

LOLA

Yes, it did. I never went home after that, but my mother
comes down here from Green Valley to visit me sometimes.

TURK

(*Bursts into the front room from outside. He is a young,
big, husky, good-looking boy, nineteen or twenty. He
has the openness, the generosity, vigor and health of
youth. He's had a little time in the service, but he is*

not what one would call disciplined. He wears faded dungarees and a T-shirt. He always enters unannounced. He hollers for MARIE.)

Hey, Marie! Ready?

MARIE

(*Calling. Runs and exits into bedroom, closing door*)
Just a minute, Turk.

LOLA

(*Confidentially*)

I'll entertain him until you're ready. (*She is by nature coy and kittenish with any attractive man. Picks up papers—stuffs them under table*) The house is such a mess, Turk! I bet you think I'm an awful housekeeper. Some day I'll surprise you. But you're like one of the family now. (*Pause*) My, you're an early caller.

TURK

Gotta get to the library. Haven't cracked a book for a biology exam and Marie's gotta help me.

LOLA

(*Unconsciously admiring his stature and physique and looking him over*)

My, I'd think you'd be chilly running around in just that thin little shirt.

TURK

Me? I go like this in the middle of winter.

LOLA

Well, you're a big husky man.

TURK

(*Laughs*)

Oh, I'm a brute, *I* am.

LOLA

You should be out in Hollywood making those Tarzan movies.

TURK

I had enough of that place when I was in the Navy.

LOLA

That so?

TURK
(*Calling*)

Hey, Marie, hurry up.

MARIE

Oh, be patient, Turk.

TURK
(*To* LOLA)

She doesn't realize how busy I am. I'll only have a half hour to study at most. I gotta report to the coach at 10:30.

LOLA

What are you in training for now?

TURK

Spring track. They got me throwing the javelin.

LOLA

The javelin? What's that?

TURK
(*Laughs at her ignorance*)

It's a big, long lance. (*Assumes the magnificent position*) You hold it like this, erect—then you let go and it goes singing through the air, and lands yards away, if you're any good at it, and sticks in the ground, quivering like an arrow. I won the State championship last year.

LOLA
(*She has watched as though fascinated*)

My!

TURK
(Very generous)

Get Marie to take you to the track field some afternoon, and you can watch me.

LOLA

That would be thrilling.

MARIE
(Comes dancing in)

Hi, Turk.

TURK

Hi, juicy.

LOLA
(As the young couple move to the doorway)

Remember, Marie, you and Turk can have the front room tonight. All to yourselves. You can play the radio and dance and make a plate of fudge, or anything you want.

MARIE
(To TURK*)*

O.K.?

TURK
(With eagerness)

Sure.

MARIE

Let's go. *(Exits.)*

LOLA

'Bye, kids.

TURK

'Bye, Mrs. Delaney. *(Gives her a chuck under the chin)* You're a swell skirt.

> *(*LOLA *couldn't be more flattered. For a moment she is breathless. They speed out the door and* LOLA *stands, sadly watching them depart. Then a sad, vacant look comes over her face. Her arms drop in a gesture of*

futility. Slowly she walks out on the front porch and calls.)

LOLA

Little Sheba! Come, Little She-ba. Come back . . . come back, Little Sheba! (*She waits for a few moments, then comes wearily back into the house, closing the door behind her. Now the morning has caught up with her. She goes to the kitchen, kicks off her pumps and gets back into comfies. The sight of the dishes on the drainboard depresses her. Clearly she is bored to death. Then the telephone rings with the promise of relieving her. She answers it*) Hello— Oh, no, you've got the wrong number— Oh, that's all right. (*Again it looks hopeless. She hears the* POSTMAN. *Now her spirits are lifted. She runs to the door, opens it and awaits him. When he's within distance, she lets loose a barrage of welcome*) 'Morning, Mr. Postman.

POSTMAN

'Morning, ma'am.

LOLA

You better have something for me today. Sometimes I think you don't even know I live here. You haven't left me anything for two whole weeks. If you can't do better than that, I'll just have to get a new postman.

POSTMAN

(*On the porch*)

You'll have to get someone to write you some letters, lady. Nope, nothing for you.

LOLA

Well, I was only joking. You knew I was joking, didn't you? I bet you're thirsty. You come right in here and I'll bring you a glass of cold water. Come in and sit down for a few minutes and rest your feet awhile.

POSTMAN

I'll take you up on that, lady. I've worked up quite a thirst.
(*Coming in.*)

LOLA

You sit down. I'll be back in just a minute.
(Goes to kitchen, gets pitcher out of refrigerator and brings it back.)

POSTMAN

Spring is turnin' into summer awful soon.

LOLA

You feel free to stop here and ask me for a drink of water any time you want to. (*Pouring drink*) That's what we're all here for, isn't it? To make each other comfortable?

POSTMAN

Thank you, ma'am.

LOLA

(Clinging, not wanting to be left alone so soon; she hurries her conversation to hold him)
You haven't been our postman very long, have you?

POSTMAN

(She pours him a glass of water, stands holding pitcher as he drinks)
No.

LOLA

You postmen have things pretty nice, don't you? I hear you get nice pensions after you been working for the government twenty years. I think that's dandy. It's a *good* job, too. (*Pours him a second glass*) You may get tired but I think it's good for a man to be outside and get a lot of exercise. Keeps him strong and healthy. My husband, he's a doctor, a *chiro*practor; he has to stay inside his office all day long. The only exercise he gets is rubbin' people's backbones. (*They laugh.* LOLA *goes* *to table, leaves pitcher*) It makes his hands strong. He's got the strongest hands you ever did see. But he's got a poor digestion. I keep tellin' him he oughta get some fresh air once in a while and some exercise. (POSTMAN *rises as if to go, and this hurries her into a more absorbing monologue*) You know what? My husband is an Alcoholics Anonymous. He doesn't care if I tell you that 'cause he's proud of it. He hasn't touched a drop in almost a year. All that time we've had a quart of whiskey in the pantry for company and he hasn't even gone near it. Doesn't even want to. You know, alcoholics can't drink like ordinary people; they're *allergic* to it. It affects them different. They get started drinking and can't stop. Liquor transforms them. Sometimes they get mean and violent and wanta fight, but if they let liquor alone, they're perfectly all right, just like you and me. (POSTMAN *tries to leave*) You should have seen Doc before he gave it up. He lost all his patients, wouldn't even go to the office; just wanted to stay drunk all day long and he'd come home at night and . . . You just wouldn't believe it if you saw him now. He's got his patients all back, and he's just doing fine.

POSTMAN

Sure, I know Dr. Delaney. I deliver his office mail. He's a fine man.

LOLA

Oh, thanks. You don't ever drink, do you?

POSTMAN

Oh, a few beers once in a while. (*He is ready to go.*)

LOLA

Well, I guess that stuff doesn't do any of us any good.

POSTMAN

No. (*Crosses down for mail on floor center*) Well, good day, ma'am.

LOLA

Say, you got any kids?

POSTMAN

Three grandchildren.

LOLA

(*Getting it from console table*)

We don't have any kids, and we got this toy in a box of breakfast food. Why don't you take it home to them?

POSTMAN

Why, that's very kind of you, ma'am. (*He takes it, and goes.*)

LOLA

Good-bye, Mr. Postman.

POSTMAN

(*On porch*)

I'll see that you get a letter, if I have to write it myself.

LOLA

Thanks. Good-bye. (*Left alone, she turns on radio. Then she goes to kitchen to start dishes, showing her boredom in the half-hearted way she washes them. Takes water back to icebox. Then she spies* MRS. COFFMAN *hanging baby clothes on lines just outside kitchen door. Goes to door*) My, you're a busy woman this morning, Mrs. Coffman.

MRS. COFFMAN

(*German accent. She is outside, but sticks her head in for some of the following*)

Being busy is being happy.

LOLA

I guess so.

MRS. COFFMAN

I don't have it as easy as you. When you got seven kids to look after, you got no time to sit around the house, Mrs. Delaney.

LOLA

I s'pose not.

MRS. COFFMAN

But you don't hear me complain.

LOLA

Oh, no. You never complain. (*Pause*) I guess my little doggie's gone for good, Mrs. Coffman. I sure miss her.

MRS. COFFMAN

The only way to keep from missing one dog is to get another.

LOLA

(*Goes to sink, turns off water*)

Oh, I never could find another doggie as cute as Little Sheba.

MRS. COFFMAN

Did you put an ad in the paper?

LOLA

For two whole weeks. No one answered it. It's just like she vanished—into thin air. (*She likes this metaphor*) Every day, though, I go out on the porch and call her. You can't tell; she might be around. Don't you think?

MRS. COFFMAN

You should get busy and forget her. You should get busy, Mrs. Delaney.

LOLA

Yes, I'm going to. I'm going to start my spring house-cleaning one of these days real soon. Why don't you come in and have a cup of coffee with me, Mrs. Coffman, and we can chat awhile?

MRS. COFFMAN

I got work to do, Mrs. Delaney. I got work. (*Exit.*)
    (LOLA *turns from the window, annoyed at her rejection. Is about to start in on the dishes when the* MILKMAN *arrives. She opens the back door and detains him.*)

MILKMAN

'Morning, Mrs. Coffman.

MRS. COFFMAN

'Morning.

LOLA

Hello there, Mr. Milkman. How are you today?

MILKMAN

'Morning, Lady.

LOLA

I think I'm going to want a few specials today. Can you come in a minute?
    (*Goes to icebox.*)

MILKMAN
(*Coming in*)

What'll it be?
    (*He probably is used to her. He is not a handsome man but husky and attractive in his uniform.*)

LOLA
(*At refrigerator*)

Well, now, let's see. You got any cottage cheese?

MILKMAN

We always got cottage cheese, Lady. (*Showing her card*)

All you gotta do is check the items on the card and we leave 'em. Now I gotta go back to the truck.

LOLA

Now, don't scold me. I always mean to do that but you're always here before I think of it. Now, I guess I'll need some coffee cream, too—half a pint.

MILKMAN

Coffee cream. O.K.

LOLA

Now let me see . . . Oh, yes, I want a quart of buttermilk. My husband has liked buttermilk ever since he stopped drinking. My husband's an alcoholic. Had to give it up. Did I ever tell you? (*Starts out. Stops at sink.*)

MILKMAN

Yes, Lady. (*Starts to go. She follows.*)

LOLA

Now he can't get enough to eat. Eats six times a day. He comes home in the middle of the morning, and I fix him a snack. In the middle of the afternoon he has a malted milk with an egg in it. And then another snack before he goes to bed.

MILKMAN

What'd ya know?

LOLA

Keeps his energy up.

MILKMAN

I'll bet. Anything else, Lady?

LOLA

No, I guess not.

MILKMAN
(Going out)
Be back in a jiffy. (*Gives her slip.*)

LOLA
I'm just so sorry I put you to so much extra work.
(*He goes. Returns shortly with dairy products.*)
After this I'm going to do my best to remember to check the
card. I don't think it's right to put people to extra work.
(*Goes to icebox, puts things away.*)

MILKMAN
(*Smiles, is willing to forget*)
That's all right, Lady.

LOLA
Maybe you'd like a piece of cake or a sandwich. Got some
awfully good cold cuts in the icebox.

MILKMAN
No, thanks, Lady.

LOLA
Or maybe you'd like a cup of coffee.

MILKMAN
No, thanks.
(*He's checking the items, putting them on the bill.*)

LOLA
You're just a young man. You oughta be going to college.
I think everyone should have an education. Do you like your
job?

MILKMAN
It's O.K. (*Looks at* LOLA.)

LOLA

You're a husky young man. You oughta be out in Hollywood making those Tarzan movies.

MILKMAN

(*Steps back. Feels a little flattered*)

When I first began on this job I didn't get enough exercise, so I started working out on the bar-bell.

LOLA

Bar-bells?

MILKMAN

Keeps you in trim.

LOLA

(*Fascinated*)

Yes, I imagine.

MILKMAN

I sent my picture in to *Strength and Health* last month. (*Proudly*) It's a physique study! If they print it, I'll bring you a copy.

LOLA

Oh, will you? I think we should all take better care of ourselves, don't you?

MILKMAN

If you ask me, Lady, that's what's wrong with the world today. We're not taking care of ourselves.

LOLA

I wouldn't be surprised.

MILKMAN

Every morning, I do forty push-ups before I eat my breakfast.

LOLA

Push-ups?

MILKMAN

Like this.

(*He spreads himself on the floor and demonstrates, doing three rapid push-ups.* LOLA *couldn't be more fascinated. Then he springs to his feet*)

That's good for shoulder development. Wanta feel my shoulders?

LOLA

Why . . . why, yes. (*He makes one arm tense and puts her hand on his shoulder*) Why, it's just like a rock.

MILKMAN

I can do seventy-nine without stopping.

LOLA

Seventy-nine!

MILKMAN

Now feel my arm.

LOLA

(*Does so*)

Goodness!

MILKMAN

You wouldn't believe what a puny kid I was. Sickly, no appetite.

LOLA

Is that a fact? And, my! Look at you now.

MILKMAN

(*Very proud*)

Shucks, any man could do the same . . . if he just takes care of himself.

LOLA

Oh, sure, sure.

(*A horn is heard offstage.*)

MILKMAN

There's my buddy. I gotta beat it. (*Picks up his things, shakes hands, leaves hurriedly*) See you tomorrow, Lady.

LOLA

'Bye.

(*She watches him from kitchen window until he gets out of sight. There is a look of some wonder on her face, an emptiness, as though she were unable to understand anything that ever happened to her. She looks at clock, runs into living room, turns on radio. A pulsating tom-tom is heard as a theme introduction. Then the* AN-NOUNCER.)

ANNOUNCER

(*In dramatic voice*)

TA-BOOoooo!

(*Now in a very soft, highly personalized voice.* LOLA *sits on couch, eats candy*)

It's Ta-boo, radio listeners, your fifteen minutes of temp*ta*tion. (*An alluring voice*) Won't you join me?

(LOLA *swings feet up*)

Won't you leave behind your routine, the dull cares that make up your day-to-day existence, the little worries, the uncertainties, the confusions of the work-a-day world and follow me where pagan spirits hold sway, where lithe natives dance on a moon-enchanted isle, where palm trees sway with the restless ocean tide, restless surging on the white shore? Won't you come along?

(*More tom-tom*)

(*Now in an oily voice*)

But remember, it's TA-BOOOOOooooo-OOO!

(*Now the tom-tom again, going into a sensual, primitive rhythm melody.* LOLA *has been transfixed from the beginning of the program. She lies down on the daven-*

port, listening, then slowly, growing more and more comfortable.)

WESTERN UNION BOY
(*At door*)
Telegram for Miss Marie Buckholder.

LOLA
She's not here.

WESTERN UNION BOY
Sign here.
(LOLA *does, then she closes the door and brings the envelope into the house, looking at it wonderingly. This is a major temptation for her. She puts the envelope on the table but can't resist looking at it. Finally she gives in and takes it to the kitchen to steam it open. Then* MARIE *and* TURK *burst into the room.* LOLA, *confused, wonders what to do with the telegram, then decides, just in the nick of time, to jam it in her apron pocket.*)

MARIE
Mrs. Delaney!
(*Turns off radio. At the sound of* MARIE'S *voice,* LOLA *embarrassedly slips the message into her pocket and runs in to greet them*)
Mind if we turn your parlor into an art studio?

LOLA
Sure, go right ahead. Hi, Turk.
(TURK *gives a wave of his arm.*)

MARIE
(*To* TURK, *indicating her bedroom*)
You can change in there, Turk. (*Exit to bedroom.*)

LOLA
(*Puzzled*)

Change?

MARIE

He's gotta take off his clothes.

LOLA

Huh?
(*Closes door.*)

MARIE

These drawings are for my life class.

LOLA
(*Consoled but still mystified*)

Oh.

MARIE
(*Sits on couch*)

Turk's the best male model we've had all year. Lotsa athletes pose for us 'cause they've all got muscles. They're easier to draw.

LOLA

You mean . . . he's gonna pose *naked*?

MARIE
(*Laughs*)

No. The women do, but the men are always more proper. Turk's going to pose in his track suit.

LOLA

Oh. (*Almost to herself*) The women pose naked but the men don't. (*This strikes her as a startling inconsistency*) If it's all right for a woman, it oughta be for a man.

MARIE
(*Businesslike*)

The man always keeps covered. (*Calling to* TURK) Hurry up, Turk.

TURK

(With all his muscles in place, he comes out. He is not at all self-conscious about his semi-nudity. His body is something he takes very much for granted. LOLA *is a little dazed by the spectacle of flesh)*

How do you want this lovely body? Same pose I took in Art Class?

MARIE

Yah. Over there where I can get more light on you.

TURK

(Opens door. Starts pose)

Anything in the house I can use for a javelin?

MARIE

Is there, Mrs. Delaney?

LOLA

How about the broom?

TURK

O.K.

*(*LOLA *runs out to get it.* TURK *goes to her in kitchen, takes it, returns to living room and resumes pose.)*

MARIE

(From her sofa, studying TURK *in relation to her sketch-pad, moves his leg)*

Your left foot a little more this way. *(Studying it)* O.K., hold it.

(Starts sketching rapidly and industriously. LOLA *looks on, lingeringly.)*

LOLA

(Starts unwillingly into kitchen, changes her mind and returns to the scene of action. MARIE *and* TURK *are too busy to comment.* LOLA *looks at sketch, inspecting it)*

Well . . . that's real pretty, Marie.

(MARIE *is intent.* LOLA *moves closer to look at the drawing*)

It . . . it's real artistic. (*Pause*) I wish *I* was artistic.

TURK

Baby, I can't hold this pose very long at a time.

MARIE

Rest whenever you feel like it.

TURK

O.K.

MARIE

(*To* LOLA)

If I make a good drawing, they'll use it for the posters for the Spring Relays.

LOLA

Ya. You told me.

MARIE

(*To* TURK)

After I'm finished with these sketches I won't have to bother you any more.

TURK

No bother. (*Rubs his shoulder—he poses*) Hard pose, though. Gets me in the shoulder.

(MARIE *pays no attention.* LOLA *peers at him so closely, he becomes a little self-conscious and breaks pose. This also breaks* LOLA's *concentration.*)

LOLA

I'll heat you up some coffee. (*Goes to kitchen.*)

TURK

(*Softly to* MARIE)

Hey, can't you keep her out of here? She makes me feel naked.

MARIE
(*Laughs*)
I can't keep her out of her own house, can I?

TURK
Didn't she ever see a man before?

MARIE
Not a big, beautiful man like you, Turky.
(TURK *smiles, is flattered by any recognition of his physical worth, takes it as an immediate invitation to lovemaking. Pulling her up, he kisses her as* DOC *comes up on porch.* MARIE *pushes* TURK *away*)
Turk, get back in your corner.
(DOC *comes in from outside.*)

DOC
(*Cheerily*)
Hi, everyone.

MARIE
Hi.

TURK
Hi, Doc. (DOC *then sees* TURK, *feels immediate resentment. Goes into kitchen to* LOLA) What's goin' on here?

LOLA
(*Getting cups*)
Oh, hello, Daddy. Marie's doin' a drawin'.

DOC
(*Trying to size up the situation.* MARIE *and* TURK *are too busy to speak*)
Oh.

LOLA
I've just heated up the coffee, want some?

DOC

Yeah. What happened to Turk's clothes?

LOLA

Marie's doing some drawings for her *life* class, Doc.

DOC

Can't she draw him with his clothes on?

LOLA

(*With coffee. Very professional now*)

No, Doc, it's not the same. See, it's a *life* class. They draw bodies. They all do it, right in the classroom.

DOC

Why, Marie's just a young girl; she shouldn't be drawing things like that. I don't care if they do teach it at college. It's not right.

LOLA

(*Disclaiming responsibility*)

I don't know, Doc.

TURK

(*Turns*)

I'm tired.

MARIE

(*Squats at his feet*)

Just let me finish the foot.

DOC

Why doesn't she draw something else, a bowl of flowers or a cathedral . . . or a sunset?

LOLA

All she told me, Doc, was if she made a good drawing of Turk, they'd use it for the posters for the Spring Relay. (*Pause*) So I guess they don't want sunsets.

DOC

What if someone walked into the house now? What would they think?

LOLA

Daddy, Marie just asked me if it was all right if Turk came and posed for her. Now that's all she said, and I said O.K. But if you think it's wrong I won't let them do it again.

DOC

I just don't like it.

MARIE

Hold it a minute more.

TURK

O.K.

LOLA

Well, then you speak to Marie about it if . . .

DOC

(*He'd never mention anything disapprovingly to* MARIE) No, Baby. I couldn't do that.

LOLA

Well, then . . .

DOC

Besides, it's not her fault. If those college people make her do drawings like that, I suppose she has to do them. I just don't think it's right she should have to, that's all.

LOLA

Well, if you think it's wrong . . .

DOC

(*Ready to dismiss it*)

Never mind.

LOLA

I don't see any harm in it, Daddy.

DOC

Forget it.

LOLA
                    (*Goes to icebox*)
Would you like some buttermilk?

DOC

Thanks.
          (MARIE *finishes sketch.*)

MARIE

O.K. That's all I can do for today.

TURK

Is there anything I can do for *you?*

MARIE

Yes—get your clothes on.

TURK

O.K., coach.
          (TURK *exits.*)

LOLA

You know what Marie said, Doc? She said that the women
pose naked, but the men don't.

DOC

Why, of course, honey.

LOLA

Why is that?

DOC
                    (*Stumped*)

Well . . .

LOLA

If it's all right for a woman it oughta be for a man. But the man always keeps covered. That's what she said.

DOC

Well, that's the way it should be, honey. A man, after all, is a man, and he . . . well, he has to protect himself.

LOLA

And a woman doesn't?

DOC

It's different, honey.

LOLA

Is it? I've got a secret, Doc. Bruce is comin'.

DOC

Is that so?

LOLA

(*After a glum silence*)

You know Marie's boy friend from Cincinnati. I promised Marie a long time ago, when her fiancé came to town, dinner was on me. So I'm getting out the best china and cooking the best meal you ever sat down to.

DOC

When did she get the news?

LOLA

The telegram came this morning.

DOC

That's fine. That Bruce sounds to me like just the fellow for her. I think I'll go in and congratulate her.

LOLA
(*Nervous*)

Not now, Doc.

DOC

Why not?

LOLA

Well, Turk's there. It might make him feel embarrassed.

DOC

Well, why doesn't Turk clear out now that Bruce is coming? What's he hanging around for? She's engaged to marry Bruce, isn't she?

> (TURK *enters from bedroom and goes to* MARIE, *starting to make advances.*)

LOLA

Marie's just doing a picture of him, Doc.

DOC

You always stick up for him. You encourage him.

LOLA

Shhh, Daddy. Don't get upset.

DOC
(*Very angrily*)

All right, but if anything happens to the girl I'll never forgive you.

> (DOC *goes upstairs.* TURK *then grabs* MARIE, *kisses her passionately.*)

Curtain

Scene II

The same evening, after supper. Outside it is dark. There has been an almost miraculous transformation of the entire house. LOLA, *apparently, has been working hard and fast all day. The rooms are spotlessly clean and there are such additions as new lampshades, fresh curtains, etc. In the kitchen all the enamel surfaces glisten, and piles of junk that have lain around for months have been disposed of.* LOLA *and* DOC *are in the kitchen, he washing up the dishes and she puttering around putting the finishing touches on her housecleaning.*

LOLA
(*At stove*)
There's still some beans left. Do you want them, Doc?

DOC
I had enough.

LOLA
I hope you got enough to eat tonight, Daddy. I been so busy cleaning I didn't have time to fix you much.

DOC
I wasn't very hungry.

LOLA
(*At table, cleaning up*)
You know what? Mrs. Coffman said I could come over and pick all the lilacs I wanted for my centerpiece tomorrow. Isn't that nice? I don't think she poisoned Little Sheba, do you?

DOC

I never did think so, Baby. Where'd you get the new curtains?

LOLA

I went out and bought them this afternoon. Aren't they pretty? Be careful of the woodwork, it's been varnished.

DOC

How come, honey?

LOLA

(Gets broom and dustpan from closet)
Bruce is comin'. I figured I had to do my spring house-cleaning some time.

DOC

You got all this done in one day? The house hasn't looked like this in years.

LOLA

I can be a good housekeeper when I want to be, can't I, Doc?

DOC

(Holding dustpan for LOLA*)*
I never had any complaints. Where's Marie now?

LOLA

I don't know, Doc. I haven't seen her since she left here this morning with Turk.

DOC

(With a look of disapproval)
Marie's too nice to be wasting her time with him.

LOLA

Daddy, Marie can take care of herself. Don't worry.
(Returns broom to closet.)

DOC

(*Goes into living room*)
'Bout time for Fibber McGee and Molly.

LOLA

(*Untying apron. Goes to closet and then back door*)
Daddy, I'm gonna run over to Mrs. Coffman's and see if
she's got any silver polish. I'll be right back.
(DOC *goes to radio.* LOLA *exits*)
(*At the radio* DOC *starts twisting the dial. He rejects one
noisy program after another, then very unexpectedly he
comes across a rendition of Shubert's famous "Ave
Maria," sung in a high soprano voice. Probably he has
encountered the piece before somewhere, but it is now
making its first impression on him. Gradually he is
transported into a world of ethereal beauty which he
never knew existed. He listens intently. The music has
expressed some ideal of beauty he never fully realized
and he is even a little mystified. Then* LOLA *comes in
the back door, letting it slam, breaking the spell, and
announcing in a loud, energetic voice:*)
Isn't it funny? I'm not a bit tired tonight. You'd think after
working so hard all day I'd be pooped.

DOC

(*In the living room; he cringes*)
Baby, don't use that word.

LOLA

(*To* DOC *on couch. Sets silver polish down and joins* DOC)
I'm sorry, Doc. I hear Marie and Turk say it all the time,
and I thought it was kinda cute.

DOC

It . . . it sounds vulgar.

LOLA

(*Kisses* DOC)

I won't say it again, Daddy. Where's Fibber McGee?

DOC

Not quite time yet.

LOLA

Let's get some peppy music.

DOC

(*Tuning in a sentimental dance band*)

That what you want?

LOLA

That's O.K. (DOC *takes a pack of cards off radio and starts shuffling them, very deftly*) I love to watch you shuffle cards, Daddy. You use your hands so gracefully. (*She watches closely*) Do me one of your card tricks.

DOC

Baby, you've seen them all.

LOLA

But I never get tired of them.

DOC

O.K. Take a card. (LOLA *does*) Keep it now. Don't tell me what it is.

LOLA

I won't.

DOC

(*Shuffling cards again*)

Now put it back in the deck. I won't look. (*He closes his eyes.*)

LOLA

(*With childish delight*)

All right.

DOC

Put it back.

LOLA

Uh-huh.

DOC

O.K. (*Shuffles cards again, cutting them, taking top half off, exposing* LOLA's *card, to her astonishment*) That your card?

LOLA

(*Unbelievingly*)

Daddy, how did you do it?

DOC

Baby, I've pulled that trick on you dozens of times.

LOLA

But I never understand how you do it.

DOC

Very simple.

LOLA

Docky, show me how you do that.

DOC

(*You can forgive him a harmless feeling of superiority*)

Try it for yourself.

LOLA

Doc, you're clever. I never could do it.

DOC

Nothing to it.

LOLA

There is *too*. Show me how you do it, Doc.

DOC

And give away all my secrets? It's a gift, honey. A magic gift.

LOLA

Can't you give it to me?

DOC

(*Picks up newspaper*)

A man has to keep some things to himself.

LOLA

It's not a gift at all, it's just some trick you *learned*.

DOC

O.K., Baby, any way you want to look at it.

LOLA

Let's have some music. How soon do you have to meet Ed Anderson?

(DOC *turns on radio.*)

DOC

I still got a little time. (*Pleased.*)

LOLA

Marie's going to be awfully happy when she sees the house all fixed up. She can entertain Bruce here when he comes, and maybe we could have a little party here and you can do your card tricks.

DOC

O.K.

LOLA

I think a young girl should be able to bring her friends home.

DOC

Sure.

LOLA

We never liked to sit around the house 'cause the folks always stayed there with us. (*Rises—starts dancing alone*) Remember the dances we used to go to, Daddy?

DOC

Sure.

LOLA

We had awful good times—for a while, didn't we?

DOC

Yes, Baby.

LOLA

Remember the homecoming dance, when Charlie Kettle-kamp and I won the Charleston contest?

DOC

Please, honey, I'm trying to read.

LOLA

And you got mad at him 'cause he thought he should take me home afterwards.

DOC

I did not.

LOLA

Yes, you did— Charlie was all right, Doc, really he was. You were just jealous.

DOC

I *wasn't* jealous.

LOLA

(She has become very coy and flirtatious now, an old dog playing old tricks)
You got jealous every time we went out any place and I even looked at another boy. There was never anything between Charlie and me; there never was.

DOC

That was a long time ago . . .

LOLA

Lots of other boys called me up for dates . . . Sammy Knight . . . Hand Biderman . . . Dutch McCoy.

DOC

Sure, Baby. You were the "it" girl.

LOLA

(*Pleading for his attention now*)
But I saved all my dates for *you*, didn't I, Doc?

DOC

(*Trying to joke*)
As far as *I* know, Baby.

LOLA

(*Hurt*)
Daddy, I did. You *got* to believe that. I never took a date with any other boy but you.

DOC

(*A little weary and impatient*)
That's all forgotten now. (*Turns off radio.*)

LOLA

How can you talk that way, Doc? That was the happiest time of our lives. I'll never forget it.

DOC

(*Disapprovingly*)
Honey!

LOLA

(*At the window*)
That was a nice spring. The trees were so heavy and green and the air smelled so sweet. Remember the walks we used to take, down to the old chapel, where it was so quiet and still? (*Sits on couch.*)

DOC

In the spring a young man's fancy turns . . . pretty fancy.

LOLA

(*In the same tone of reverie*)

I was pretty then, wasn't I, Doc? Remember the first time you kissed me? You were scared as a young girl, I believe, Doc; you trembled so. (*She is being very soft and delicate. Caught in the reverie, he chokes a little and cannot answer*) We'd been going together all year and you were always so shy. Then for the first time you grabbed me and kissed me. Tears came to your eyes, Doc, and you said you'd love me forever and ever. Remember? You said . . . if I didn't marry you, you wanted to die . . . I remember 'cause it scared me for anyone to say a thing like that.

DOC

(*In a repressed tone*)

Yes, Baby.

LOLA

And when the evening came on, we stretched out on the cool grass and you kissed me all night long.

DOC

(*Opens doors*)

Baby, you've got to forget those things. That was twenty years ago.

LOLA

I'll soon be forty. Those years have just vanished vanished into thin air.

DOC

Yes.

LOLA

Just disappeared—like Little Sheba. (*Pause*) Maybe you're

sorry you married me now. You didn't know I was going to get old and fat and sloppy . . .

DOC

Oh, Baby!

LOLA

It's the truth. That's what I am. But I didn't know it, either. Are you sorry you married me, Doc?

DOC

Of course not.

LOLA

I mean, are you sorry you *had* to marry me?

DOC

(*Goes to porch*)

We were never going to talk about that, Baby.

LOLA

(*Following* DOC *out*)

You *were* the first one, Daddy, the *only* one. I'd just die if you didn't believe that.

DOC

(*Tenderly*)

I know, Baby.

LOLA

You were so nice and so proper, Doc; I thought nothing we could do together could ever be wrong—or make us unhappy. Do you think we did wrong, Doc?

DOC

(*Consoling*)

No, Baby, of course I don't.

LOLA

I don't think anyone knows about it except my folks, do you?

DOC

Of course not, Baby.

LOLA

(*Follows him in*)

I wish the baby had lived, Doc. I don't think that woman knew her business, do you, Doc?

DOC

I guess not.

LOLA

If we'd gone to a doctor, she would have lived, don't you think?

DOC

Perhaps.

LOLA

A doctor wouldn't have known we'd just got married, would he? Why were we so afraid?

DOC

(*Sits on couch*)

We were just kids. Kids don't know how to look after things.

LOLA

(*Sits on couch*)

If we'd had the baby she'd be a young girl now; then maybe you'd have saved your money, Doc, and she could be going to college—like Marie.

DOC

Baby, what's done is done.

LOLA

It must make you feel bad at times to think you had to

give up being a doctor and to think you don't have any money like you used to.

DOC

No . . . no, Baby. We should never feel bad about what's past. What's in the past can't be helped. You . . . you've got to forget it and live for the present. If you can't forget the past, you stay in it and never get out. I might be a big M.D. today, instead of a chiropractor; we might have had a family to raise and be with us now; I might still have a lot of money if I'd used my head and invested it carefully, instead of gettin' drunk every night. We might have a nice house, and comforts, and friends. But we don't have any of those things. So what! We gotta keep on living, don't we? I can't stop just 'cause I made a few mistakes. I gotta keep goin' . . . somehow.

LOLA

Sure, Daddy.

DOC

(*Sighs and wipes brow*)

I . . . I wish you wouldn't ask me questions like that, Baby. Let's not talk about it any more. I gotta keep goin', and not let things upset me, or . . . or . . . *I* saw enough at the City Hospital to keep me sober for a long time.

LOLA

I'm sorry, Doc. I didn't mean to upset you.

DOC

I'm not upset.

LOLA

What time'll you be home tonight?

DOC

'Bout eleven o'clock.

LOLA

I wish you didn't have to go tonight. I feel kinda lonesome.

DOC

Ya, so am I, Baby, but some time soon, we'll go *out* together. I kinda hate to go to those night clubs and places since I stopped drinking, but some night I'll take you out to dinner.

LOLA

Oh, will you, Daddy?

DOC

We'll get dressed up and go to the Windermere and have a fine dinner and dance between courses.

LOLA

(*Eagerly*)

Let's do, Daddy. I got a little money saved up. I got about forty dollars out in the kitchen. We can take that if you need it.

DOC

I'll have plenty of money the first of the month.

LOLA

(*She has made a quick response to the change of mood, seeing a future evening of carefree fun.*) What are we sitting round here so serious for? (*Turns to radio*) Let's have some music. (LOLA *gets a lively foxtrot on the radio, dances with* DOC. *They begin dancing vigorously as though to dispense with the sadness of the preceding dialogue, but slowly it winds them and leaves* LOLA *panting*) We oughta go dancing . . . all the time, Docky . . . It'd be good for us. Maybe if I danced more often, I'd lose . . . some of . . . this fat. I remember . . . I used to be able to dance like this . . . all night . . . and not even notice . . . it. (LOLA *breaks into a Charleston routine as of yore*) Remember the Charleston, Daddy?

(DOC *is clapping his hands in rhythm. Then* MARIE *bursts in through the front door, the personification of the youth that* LOLA *is trying to recapture.*)

DOC

Hi, Marie.

MARIE

What are you trying to do, a jig, Mrs. Delaney?

(MARIE *doesn't intend her remark to be cruel, but it wounds* LOLA. LOLA *stops abruptly in her dancing, losing all the fun she has been able to create for herself. She feels she might cry; so to hide her feelings she hurries quietly out to kitchen, but* DOC *and* MARIE *do not notice.* MARIE *notices the change in atmosphere*)

Hey, what's been happening around here?

DOC

Lola got to feeling industrious. You oughta see the kitchen.

MARIE

(*Running to kitchen, where she is too observant of the changes to notice* LOLA *weeping in corner.* LOLA, *of course, straightens up as soon as* MARIE *enters*)

What got into you, Mrs. Delaney? You've done wonders with the house. It looks marvelous.

LOLA

(*Quietly*)

Thanks, Marie.

MARIE

(*Darting back into living room*)

I can hardly believe I'm in the same place.

DOC

Think your boy friend'll like it? (*Meaning* BRUCE.)

MARIE

(*Thinking of* TURK)

You know how men are. Turk never notices things like that. (*Starts into her room blowing a kiss to* DOC *on her way.* LOLA *comes back in, dabbing at her eyes.*)

DOC

Turk? (MARIE *is gone; he turns to* LOLA) What's the matter, honey?

LOLA

I don't know.

DOC

Feel bad about something?

LOLA

I didn't want her to see me dancing that way. Makes me feel sorta silly.

DOC

Why, you're a fine dancer.

LOLA

I feel kinda silly.

MARIE

(*Jumps back into the room with her telegram*)

My telegram's here. When did it come?

LOLA

It came about an hour ago, honey.

(LOLA *looks nervously at* DOC. DOC *looks puzzled and a little sore.*)

MARIE

Bruce is coming! "Arriving tomorrow 5:00 P.M. CST, Flight 22, Love, Bruce." When did the telegram come?

DOC
(*Looking hopelessly at* LOLA)
So it came an hour ago.

LOLA
(*Nervously*)
Isn't it nice I got the house all cleaned? Marie, you bring Bruce to dinner with us tomorrow night. It'll be a sort of wedding present.

MARIE
That would be wonderful, Mrs. Delaney, but I don't want you to go to any trouble.

LOLA
No trouble at all. Now I insist. (*Front doorbell rings*) That must be Turk.

MARIE
(*Whisper*)
Don't tell *him*. (*Goes to door.* LOLA *scampers to kitchen*) Hi, Turk. Come on in.

TURK
(*Entering. Stalks her*)
Hi.
(*Looks around to see if anyone is present, then takes her in his arms and starts to kiss her.*)

LOLA
I'm sorry, Doc. I'm sorry about the telegram.

DOC
Baby, people don't do things like that. Don't you understand? *Nice* people don't.

MARIE
Stop it!

TURK
What's the matter?

COME BACK, LITTLE SHEBA

MARIE

They're in the kitchen.
(TURK *sits with book.*)

DOC

Why didn't you give it to her when it came?

LOLA

Turk was posing for Marie this morning and I couldn't
give it to her while he was here.
(TURK *listens at door.*)

DOC

Well, it just isn't nice to open other people's mail.
(TURK *goes to* MARIE's *door.*)

LOLA

I guess I'm not nice then. That what you mean?

MARIE

Turk, will you get away from that door?

DOC

No, Baby, but . . .

LOLA

I don't see any harm in it, Doc. I steamed it open and sealed
it back. (TURK *at switch in living room*) She'll never know
the difference. I don't see any harm in that, Doc.

DOC
(*Gives up*)
O.K., Baby, if you don't see any harm in it, I guess I can't
explain it.
(*Starts getting ready to go.*)

LOLA

I'm sorry, Doc. Honest, I'll never do it again. Will you forgive me?

DOC
(*Giving her a peck of a kiss*)
I forgive you.

MARIE
(*Comes back with book*)
Let's look like we're studying.

TURK

Biology? Hot dog!

LOLA
(*After* MARIE *leaves her room*)
Now I feel better. Do you have to go now?
(TURK *sits by* MARIE *on the couch.*)

DOC

Yah.

LOLA

Before you go, why don't you show your tricks to Marie?

DOC
(*Reluctantly*)
Not now.

LOLA

Oh, please do. They'd be crazy about them.

DOC
(*With pride*)
O.K. (*Preens himself a little*) If you think they'd enjoy
them . . .
(LOLA, *starting to living room, stops suddenly upon
seeing* MARIE *and* TURK *spooning behind a book. A*

broad, pleased smile breaks on her face and she stands silently watching. DOC *is at sink*)
Well . . . what's the matter, Baby?

LOLA
(*In a soft voice*)
Oh . . . nothing . . . nothing . . . Doc.

DOC
Well, do you want me to show 'em my tricks or don't you?

LOLA
(*Coming back to center kitchen; in a secretive voice with a little giggle*)
I guess they wouldn't be interested now.

DOC
(*With injured pride. A little sore*)
Oh, very well.

LOLA
Come and look, Daddy.

DOC
(*Shocked and angry*)
No!

LOLA
Just one little look. They're just kids, Daddy. It's sweet.
(*Drags him by arm.*)

DOC
(*Jerking loose*)
Stop it, Baby. I won't do it. It's not decent to snoop around spying on people like that. It's cheap and mischievous and mean.

LOLA
(*This had never occurred to her*)
Is it?

DOC
Of course it is.

LOLA
I don't spy on Marie and Turk to be mischievous and mean.

DOC
Then why *do* you do it?

LOLA
You watch young people make love in the movies, don't you, Doc? There's nothing wrong with that. And I *know* Marie and I like her, and Turk's nice, too. They're both so young and pretty. Why shouldn't I watch them?

DOC
I give up.

LOLA
Well, why shouldn't I?

DOC
I don't know, Baby, but it's not nice.
(TURK *kisses* MARIE's *ear.*)

LOLA
(*Plaintive*)
I think it's one of the nicest things I know.

MARIE
Let's go out on the porch.
(*They steal out.*)

DOC
It's not right for Marie to do that, particularly since Bruce is coming. We shouldn't allow it.

LOLA

Oh, they don't do any harm, Doc. I think it's all right.
(TURK *and* MARIE *go to porch*.)

DOC

It's not all right. I don't know why you encourage that sort
of thing.

LOLA

I don't encourage it.

DOC

You do, too. You like that fellow Turk. You said so. And
I say he's no good. Marie's sweet and innocent; she doesn't
understand guys like him. I think I oughta run him outa the
house.

LOLA

Daddy, you wouldn't do that.

DOC

(*Very heated*)
Then you talk to her and tell her how we feel.

LOLA

Hush, Daddy. They'll hear you.

DOC

I don't care if they do hear me.

LOLA

(*To* DOC *at stove*)
Don't get upset, Daddy. Bruce is coming and Turk won't
be around any longer. I promise you.

DOC

All right. I better go.

LOLA

I'll go with you, Doc. Just let me run up and get a sweater.
Now wait for me.

DOC

Hurry, Baby.

(LOLA *goes upstairs.* DOC *is at platform when he hears* TURK *laugh on the porch.* DOC *sees whisky bottle. Reaches for it and hears* MARIE *giggle. Turns away as* TURK *laughs again. Turns back to the bottle and hears* LOLA's *voice from upstairs.*)

LOLA

I'll be there in a minute, Doc. (*Enters downstairs*) I'm all ready. (DOC *turns out kitchen lights and they go into living room*) I'm walking Doc down to the bus. (DOC *sees* TURK *with* LOLA's *picture. Takes it out of his hand, puts it on shelf as* LOLA *leads him out.* DOC *is offstage*) Then I'll go for a long walk in the moonlight. Have a good time. (*She exits.*)

MARIE

'Bye, Mrs. Delaney. (*Exits.*)

TURK

He hates my guts. (*Goes to front door.*)

MARIE

Oh, he does not. (*Follows* TURK, *blocks his exit in door.*)

TURK

Yes, he does. If you ask me, he's jealous.

MARIE

Jealous?

TURK

I've always thought he had a crush on you.

MARIE

Now, Turk, don't be silly. Doc is nice to me. It's just in a few little things he does, like fixing my breakfast, but he's nice to everyone.

TURK

He ever make a pass?

MARIE

No. He'd never get fresh.

TURK

He better not.

MARIE

Turk, don't be ridiculous. Doc's such a nice, quiet man; if he gets any fun out of being nice to me, why not?

TURK

He's got a wife of his own, hasn't he? Why doesn't he make a few passes at her?

MARIE

Things like that are none of our business.

TURK

O.K. How about a snuggle, lovely?

MARIE

(*A little prim and businesslike*)
No more for tonight, Turk.

TURK

Why's tonight different from any other night?

MARIE

I think we should make it a rule, every once in a while, just to sit and talk.
    (*Starts to sit on couch, but goes to chair.*)

TURK

(*Restless, sits on couch*)
O.K. What'll we talk about?

MARIE

Well . . . there's lotsa things.

TURK

O.K. Start in.

MARIE

A person doesn't start a conversation that way.

TURK

Start it any way you want to.

MARIE

Two people should have something to talk about, like politics or psychology or religion.

TURK

How 'bout sex?

MARIE

Turk!

TURK
(*Chases her around couch*)
Have you read the Kinsey Report, Miss Buckholder?

MARIE

I should say not.

TURK

How old were you when you had your first affair, Miss Buckholder? And did you ever have relations with your grandfather?

MARIE

Turk, stop it.

TURK

You wanted to talk about something; I was only trying to please. Let's have a kiss.

MARIE

Not tonight.

TURK

Who you savin' it up for?

MARIE

Don't talk that way.

TURK

(*Gets up, yawns*)

Well, thanks, Miss Buckholder, for a nice evening. It's been a most enjoyable talk.

MARIE

(*Anxious*)

Turk, where are you going?

TURK

I guess I'm a man of action, Baby.

MARIE

Turk, don't go.

TURK

Why not? I'm not doin' any good here.

MARIE

Don't go.

TURK

(*Returns and she touches him. They sit on couch*)

Now why didn't you think of this before? C'mon, let's get to work.

MARIE

Oh, Turk, this is all we ever do.

TURK

Are you complaining?

MARIE

(*Weakly*)

No.

TURK

Then what do you want to put on such a front for?

MARIE

It's not a front.

TURK

What else is it? (*Mimicking*) Oh, no, Turk. Not tonight, Turk. I want to talk about philosophy, Turk. (*Himself again*) When all the time you know that if I went outa here without givin' you a good lovin' up you'd be sore as hell . . . Wouldn't you?

MARIE

(*She has to admit to herself it's true; she chuckles*) Oh . . . Turk . . .

TURK

It's true, isn't it?

MARIE

Maybe.

TURK

How about tonight, lovely; going to be lonesome?

MARIE

Turk, you're in training.

TURK

What of it? I can throw that old javelin any old time, *any* old time. C'mon, Baby, we've got by with it before, haven't we?

MARIE

I'm not so sure.

TURK

What do you mean?

MARIE

Sometimes I think Mrs. Delaney knows.

TURK

Well, bring her along. I'll take care of her, too, if it'll keep her quiet.

MARIE

(*A pretense of being shocked*)

Turk!

TURK

What makes you think so?

MARIE

Women just sense those things. She asks so many questions.

TURK

She ever *say* anything?

MARIE

No.

TURK

Now *you're* imagining things.

MARIE

Maybe.

TURK

Well, stop it.

MARIE

O.K.

TURK

(*Follows* MARIE)

Honey, I know I talk awful rough around you at times; I never was a very gentlemanly bastard, but you really don't mind it . . . do you? (*She only smiles mischievously*) Anyway, you know I'm nuts about you.

MARIE

(*Smug*)

Are you?

(*Now they engage in a little rough-house, he cuffing her like an affectionate bear, she responding with "Stop it," "Turk, that hurt," etc. And she slaps him playfully. Then they laugh together at their own pretense. Now*

LOLA *enters the back way very quietly, tiptoeing through the dark kitchen, standing by the doorway where she can peek at them. There is a quiet, satisfied smile on her face. She watches every move they make, alertly.*)

TURK

Now, Miss Buckholder, what is your opinion of the psychodynamic pressure of living in the atomic age?

MARIE
(*Playfully*)
Turk, don't make fun of me.

TURK

Tonight?

MARIE
(*Her eyes dance as she puts him off just a little longer*)
Well.

TURK

Tonight will never come again. (*This is true. She smiles.*) O.K.?

MARIE

Tonight will never come again. . . . (*They embrace and start to dance*) Let's go out somewhere first and have a few beers. We can't come back till they're asleep.

TURK

O.K.

(*They dance slowly out the door. Then* LOLA *moves quietly into the living room and out onto the porch. There she can be heard calling plaintively in a lost voice.*)

LOLA

Little Sheba . . . Come back . . . Come back, Little Sheba. Come back.

Curtain

ACT TWO

ACT TWO

Scene I

The next morning. LOLA *and* DOC *are at breakfast again.* LOLA *is rambling on while* DOC *sits meditatively, his head down, his face in his hands.*

LOLA

(In a light, humorous way, as though the faults of youth were as blameless as the uncontrollable actions of a puppy. Chuckles.)
Then they danced for a while and went out together, arm in arm. . . .

DOC

(Sitting at table, very nervous and tense)
I don't wanta hear any more about it, Baby.

LOLA

What's the matter, Docky?

DOC

Nothing.

LOLA

You look like you didn't feel very good.

DOC

I didn't sleep well last night.

LOLA

You didn't take any of those sleeping pills, did you?

DOC

No.

LOLA

Well, don't. The doctors say they're terrible for you.

DOC

I'll feel better after a while.

LOLA

Of course you will.

DOC

What time did Marie come in last night?

LOLA

I don't know, Doc. I went to bed early and went right to sleep. Why?

DOC

Oh . . . nothing.

LOLA

You musta slept if you didn't hear her.

DOC

I heard her; it was after midnight.

LOLA

Then what did you ask me for?

DOC

I wasn't sure it was her.

LOLA

What do you mean?

DOC

I thought I heard a man's voice.

LOLA

Turk probably brought her inside the door.

DOC

(*Troubled*)

I thought I heard someone laughing. A man's laugh . . .
I guess I was just hearing things.

LOLA

Say your prayer?

DOC

(*Gets up*)

Yes.

LOLA

Kiss me 'bye. (*He leans over and kisses her, then puts on
his coat and starts to leave*) Do you think you could get home
a little early? I want you to help me entertain Bruce. Marie
said he'd be here about 5:30. I'm going to have a lovely
dinner: stuffed pork chops, twice-baked potatoes, and aspara-
gus, and for dessert a big chocolate cake and maybe ice
cream . . .

DOC

Sounds fine.

LOLA

So you get home and help me.

DOC

O.K.

(DOC *leaves kitchen and goes into living room. Again
on the chair is* MARIE's *scarf. He picks it up as before
and fondles it. Then there is the sound of* TURK's *laugh-
ter, soft and barely audible. It sounds like the laugh of
a sated Bacchus.* DOC's *body stiffens. It is a sickening fact
he must face and it has been revealed to him in its
ugliest light. The lyrical grace, the spiritual ideal of
Ave Maria is shattered. He has been fighting the truth,
maybe suspecting all along that he was deceiving himself. Now he looks as though he might vomit. All his
blind confusion is inside him. With an immobile ex-*

pression of blankness on his face, he stumbles into the table above the sofa.)

LOLA
(*Still in kitchen*)
Haven't you gone yet, Docky?

DOC
(*Dazed*)
No . . . no, Baby.

LOLA
(*In doorway*)
Anything the matter?

DOC
No . . . no. I'm all right now. (*Drops scarf, takes hat, exits. He has managed to sound perfectly natural. He braces himself and goes out.* LOLA *stands a moment, looking after him with a little curiosity. Then* MRS. COFFMAN *enters, sticks her head in back door.*)

MRS. COFFMAN
Anybody home?

LOLA
(*On platform*)
'Morning, Mrs. Coffman.

MRS. COFFMAN
(*Inspecting the kitchen's new look*)
So this is what you've been up to, Mrs. Delaney.

LOLA
(*Proud*)
Yes, I been busy.
(MARIE's *door opens and closes.* MARIE *sticks her head out of her bedroom door to see if the coast is clear, then sticks her head back in again to whisper to* TURK *that he can leave without being observed.*)

MRS. COFFMAN

Busy? Good Lord, I never seen such activity. What got into you, Lady?

LOLA

Company tonight. I thought I'd fix things up a little.

MRS. COFFMAN

You mean you done all this in one day?

LOLA

(*With simple pride*)

I said I been busy.

MRS. COFFMAN

Dear God, you done your spring house-cleaning all in one day. (TURK *appears in living room.*)

LOLA

(*Appreciating this*)

I fixed up the living room a little, too.

MRS. COFFMAN

I must see it. (*Goes into living room.* TURK *overhears her and ducks back into* MARIE's *room, shutting the door behind himself and* MARIE) I declare! Overnight you turn the place into something really swanky.

LOLA

Yes, and I bought a few new things, too.

MRS. COFFMAN

Neat as a pin, and so warm and cozy. I take my hat off to you, Mrs. Delaney. I didn't know you had it in you. All these years, now, I been sayin' to myself, "That Mrs. Delaney is a good for nothing, sits around the house all day, and never so much as shakes a dust mop." I guess it just shows, we never really know what people are like.

LOLA

I still got some coffee.

MRS. COFFMAN

Not now, Mrs. Delaney. Seeing your house so clean makes me feel ashamed. I gotta get home and get to work. (*Goes to kitchen.*)

LOLA
(*Follows*)

I hafta get busy, too. I got to get out all the silver and china. I like to set the table early, so I can spend the rest of the day looking at it.
(*Both laugh.*)

MRS. COFFMAN

Good day, Mrs. Delaney. (*Exits.*)
(*Hearing the screen door slam, MARIE guards the kitchen door and TURK slips out the front. But neither has counted on DOC's reappearance. After seeing that TURK is safe, MARIE blows a good-bye kiss to him and joins LOLA in the kitchen. But DOC is coming in the front door just as TURK starts to go out. There is a moment of blind embarrassment, during which DOC only looks stupefied and TURK, after mumbling an unintelligible apology, runs out. First DOC is mystified, trying to figure it all out. His face looks more and more troubled. Meanwhile, MARIE and LOLA are talking in the kitchen.*)

MARIE

Boo! (*Sneaking up behind LOLA at back porch.*)

LOLA
(*Jumping around*)

Heavens! You scared me, Marie. You up already?

MARIE

Yah.

LOLA

This is Saturday. You could sleep as late as you wanted.

MARIE

(*Pouring a cup of coffee*)

I thought I'd get up early and help you.

LOLA

Honey, I'd sure appreciate it. You can put up the table in the living room, after you've had your breakfast. That's where we'll eat. Then you can help me set it.

(DOC *closes door.*)

MARIE

O.K.

LOLA

Want a sweet roll?

MARIE

I don't think so. Turk and I had so much beer last night. He got kinda tight.

LOLA

He shouldn't do that, Marie.

MARIE

(*Starts for living room*)

Just keep the coffee hot for me. I'll want another cup in a minute. (*Stops on seeing* DOC) Why, Dr. Delaney! I thought you'd gone.

DOC

(*Trying to sustain his usual manner*)

Good morning, Marie. (*But not looking at her.*)

MARIE

(*She immediately wonders*)

Why . . . why . . . how long have you been here, Doc?

DOC

Just got here, just this minute.

LOLA
(*Comes in*)

That you, Daddy?

DOC

It's me.

LOLA

What are you doing back?

DOC

I . . . I just thought maybe I'd feel better . . . if I took a glass of soda water . . .

LOLA

I'm afraid you're not well, Daddy.

DOC

I'm all right. (*Starts for kitchen.*)

LOLA
(*Helping* MARIE *with table*)

The soda's on the drainboard.

> (DOC *goes to kitchen, fixes some soda, and stands a moment, just thinking. Then he sits sipping the soda, as though he were trying to make up his mind about something*)

Marie, would you help me move the table? It'd be nice now if we had a dining room, wouldn't it? But if we had a dining room, I guess we wouldn't have you, Marie. It was my idea to turn the dining room into a bedroom and rent it. I thought of lots of things to do for extra money . . . a few years ago . when Doc was so . . . so sick.

> (*They set up table*—LOLA *gets cloth from cabinet.*)

MARIE

This is a lovely tablecloth.

LOLA

Irish linen. Doc's mother gave it to us when we got married. She gave us all our silver and china, too. The china's Havelin. I'm so proud of it. It's the most valuable possession we own. I just washed it. . . . Will you help me bring it in? (*Getting china from kitchen*) Doc was sortuva Mama's boy. He was an only child and his mother thought the sun rose and set in him. Didn't she, Docky? She brought Doc up like a real gentleman.

MARIE

Where are the napkins?

LOLA

Oh, I forgot them. They're so nice I keep them in my bureau drawer with my handkerchiefs. Come upstairs and we'll get them.

> (LOLA *and* MARIE *go upstairs. Then* DOC *listens to be sure* LOLA *and* MARIE *are upstairs, looks cautiously at the whiskey bottle on pantry shelf but manages to resist several times. Finally he gives in to temptation, grabs bottle off shelf, then starts wondering how to get past* LOLA *with it. Finally, it occurs to him to wrap it inside his trench coat which he gets from pantry and carries over his arm.* LOLA *and* MARIE *are heard upstairs. They return to the living room and continue setting table as* DOC *enters from kitchen on his way out.*)

LOLA
(*Coming downstairs*)

Did you ever notice how nice he keeps his fingernails? Not many men think of things like that. And he used to take his mother to church every Sunday.

MARIE
(*At table*)

Oh, Doc's a real gentleman.

LOLA

Treats women like they were all beautiful angels. We went together a whole year before he even kissed me. (DOC *comes through the living room with coat and bottle, going to front door*) On your way back to the office now, Docky?

DOC
(*His back to them*)

Yes.

LOLA

Aren't you going to kiss me good-bye before you go, Daddy? (*She goes to him and kisses him.* MARIE *catches* DOC's *eye and smiles. Then she exits to her room, leaving door open*) Get home early as you can. I'll need you. We gotta give Bruce a royal welcome.

DOC

Yes, Baby.

LOLA

Feeling all right?

DOC

Yes.

LOLA
(*In doorway,* DOC *is on porch*)

Take care of yourself.

DOC
(*In a toneless voice*)

Good-bye. (*He goes.*)

LOLA
(*Coming back to table with pleased expression, which changes to a puzzled look, calls to* MARIE)

Now that's funny. Why did Doc take his raincoat? It's a beautiful day. There isn't a cloud in sight.

Curtain

Scene II

It is now 5:30. The scene is the same as the preceding except that more finishing touches have been added and the two women, still primping the table, lighting the tapers, are dressed in their best. LOLA *is arranging the centerpiece.*

LOLA
(*Above table, fixing flowers*)
I just love lilacs, don't you, Marie? (*Takes one and studies it*) Mrs. Coffman was nice; she let me have all I wanted. (*Looks at it very closely*) Aren't they pretty? And they smell so sweet. I think they're the nicest flower there is.

MARIE
They don't last long.

LOLA
(*Respectfully*)
No. Just a few days. Mrs. Coffman's started blooming just day before yesterday.

MARIE
By the first of the week they'll all be gone.

LOLA
Vanish . . . they'll vanish into thin air. (*Gayer now*) Here, honey, we have them to spare *now*. Put this in your hair. There. (MARIE *does*) Mrs. Coffman's been so nice lately. I didn't use to like her. Now where could Doc be? He promised he'd get here early. He didn't even come home for lunch.

MARIE
(*Gets two chairs from bedroom*)
Mrs. Delaney, you're a peach to go to all this trouble.

85

LOLA

(*Gets salt and pepper*)

Shoot, I'm gettin' more fun out of it than you are. Do you think Bruce is going to like us?

MARIE

If he doesn't, I'll never speak to him again.

LOLA

(*Eagerly*)

I'm just dying to meet him. But I feel sorta bad I never got to do anything nice for Turk.

MARIE

(*Carefully prying*)

Did . . . Doc ever say anything to you about Turk . . . and me?

LOLA

About Turk and you? No, honey. Why?

MARIE

I just wondered.

LOLA

What if Bruce finds out that you've been going with someone else?

MARIE

Bruce and I had a very businesslike understanding before I left for school that we weren't going to sit around lonely just because we were separated.

LOLA

Aren't you being kind of mean to Turk?

MARIE

I don't think so.

LOLA

How's he going to feel when Bruce comes?

MARIE

He may be sore for a little while, but he'll get over it.

LOLA

Won't he feel bad?

MARIE

He's had his eye on a pretty little Spanish girl in his history class for a long time. I like Turk, but he's not the marrying kind.

LOLA

No! Really?

(LOLA, *with a look of sad wonder on her face, sits on arm of couch. It's been a serious disillusionment.*)

MARIE

What's the matter?

LOLA

I . . . I just felt kinda tired.

(*Sharp buzzing of doorbell.* MARIE *runs to answer it.*)

MARIE

That must be Bruce. (*She skips to the mirror again, then to door*) Bruce!

BRUCE

How are you, sweetheart?

MARIE

Wonderful.

BRUCE

Did you get my wire?

MARIE

Sure.

BRUCE

You're looking swell.

MARIE

Thanks. What took you so long to get here?

BRUCE

Well, honey, I had to go to my hotel and take a bath.

MARIE

Bruce, this is Mrs. Delaney.

BRUCE

(*Now he gets the cozy quality out of his voice*)
How do you do, ma'am?

LOLA

How d'ya do?

BRUCE

Marie has said some very nice things about you in her letters.

MARIE

Mrs. Delaney has fixed the grandest dinner for us.

BRUCE

Now that was to be my treat. I have a big expense account now, honey. I thought we could all go down to the hotel and have dinner there, and celebrate first with a few cocktails.

LOLA

Oh, we can have cocktails, too. Excuse me, just a minute.
(*She hurries to the kitchen and starts looking for the whiskey.* BRUCE *kisses* MARIE.)

MARIE

(*Whispers*)
Now, Bruce, she's been working on this dinner all day. She even cleaned the house for you.

BRUCE
(With a surveying look)
Did she?

MARIE
And Doc's joining us. You'll like Doc.

BRUCE
Honey, are we going to have to stay here the whole evening?

MARIE
We just can't eat and run. We'll get away as soon as we can.

BRUCE
I hope so. I got the raise, sweetheart. They're giving me new territory.

(LOLA is frantic in the kitchen, having found the bottle missing. She hurries back into the living room.)

LOLA
You kids are going to have to entertain yourselves awhile 'cause I'm going to be busy in the kitchen. Why don't you turn on the radio, Marie? Get some dance music. I'll shut the door so . . . so I won't disturb you.

(LOLA does so, then goes to the telephone.)

MARIE
Come and see my room, Bruce. I've fixed it up just darling. And I've got your picture in the prettiest frame right on my dresser.

(They exit and their voices are heard from the bedroom while LOLA is phoning.)

LOLA
(At the phone)
This is Mrs. Delaney. Is . . . Doc there? Well, then, is Ed Anderson there? Well, would you give me Ed Anderson's

telephone number? You see, he sponsored Doc into the club and helped him . . . you know . . . and . . . and I was a little worried tonight. . . . Oh, thanks. Yes, I've got it. (*She writes down number*) Could you have Ed Anderson call me if he comes in? Thank you.

(*She hangs up. On her face is a dismal expression of fear, anxiety and doubt. She searches flour bin, icebox, closet. Then she goes into the living room, calling to* MARIE *and* BRUCE *as she comes*)

I . . . I guess we'll go ahead without Doc, Marie.

MARIE

(*Enters from her room*)
What's the matter with Doc, Mrs. Delaney?

LOLA

Well . . . he got held up at the office . . . just one of those things, you know. It's too bad. It would have to happen when I needed him most.

MARIE

Sure you don't need any help?

LOLA

Huh? Oh, no. I'll make out. Everything's ready. I tell you what I'm going to do. Three's a crowd, so I'm going to be the butler and serve the dinner to you two young lovebirds . . . (*The telephone rings*) Pardon me . . . pardon me just a minute. (*She rushes to phone, closing the door behind her*) Hello? Ed? Have you seen Doc? He went out this morning and hasn't come back. We're having company for dinner and he was supposed to be home early. . . . That's not all. This time we've had a quart of whiskey in the kitchen and Doc's never gone near it. I went to get it tonight. I was going to serve some cocktails. It was *gone*. Yes, I saw it there yesterday. No, I don't think so. . . . He said this morning he had an upset stomach but . . . Oh, would you? . . . Thank you, Mr. Anderson. Thank you a million times. And you let me know when you find out anything. Yes, I'll be here . . . yes. (*Hangs up and crosses back to living room*) Well, I guess we're all ready.

BRUCE

Aren't you going to look at your present?

MARIE

Oh, sure, let's get some scissors.
(*Their voices continue in bedroom.*)

MARIE

(*Enters with* BRUCE)
Mrs. Delaney, we think you should eat with us.

LOLA

Oh, no, honey, I'm not very hungry. Besides, this is the first time you've been together in months and I think you should be alone. Marie, why don't you light the candles? Then we'll have just the right atmosphere.
(*She goes into kitchen, gets tomato-juice glasses from icebox while* BRUCE *lights the candles.*)

BRUCE

Do we have to eat by candlelight? I won't be able to see.
(LOLA *returns.*)

LOLA

Now, Bruce, you sit here. (*He and* MARIE *sit*) Isn't that going to be cozy? Dinner for two. Sorry we won't have time for cocktails. Let's have a little music. (*She turns on the radio and a Viennese waltz swells up as the curtain falls with* LOLA *looking at the young people eating.*)

Curtain

Scene III

Funereal atmosphere. It is about 5:30 the next morning. The sky is just beginning to get light outside, while inside the room the shadows still cling heavily to the corners. The remains of last night's dinner clutter the table in the living room. The candles have guttered down to stubs amid the dirty dinner plates, and the lilacs in the centerpiece have wilted. LOLA *is sprawled on the davenport, sleeping. Slowly she awakens and regards the morning light. She gets up and looks about strangely, beginning to show despair for the situation she is in. She wears the same spiffy dress she had on the night before but it is wrinkled now, and her marcelled coiffure is awry. One silk stocking has twisted loose and falls around her ankle. When she is sufficiently awake to realize her situation, she rushes to the telephone and dials a number.*

LOLA

(At telephone. She sounds frantic)

Mr. Anderson? Mr. Anderson, this is Mrs. Delaney again. I'm sorry to call you so early, but I just *had* to. . . . Did you find Doc? . . . No, he's not home yet. I don't suppose he'll come home till he's drunk all he can hold and wants to sleep. . . . I don't know what else to think, Mr. Anderson. I'm scared, Mr. Anderson. I'm awful scared. Will you come right over? . . . Thanks, Mr. Anderson.

(She hangs up and goes to kitchen to make coffee. She finds some left from the night before, so turns on the fire to warm it up. She wanders around vaguely, trying to get her thoughts in order, jumping at every sound. Pours herself a cup of coffee, then takes it to living

92

room, sits and sips it. Very quietly DOC *enters through
the back way into the kitchen. He carries a big bottle
of whiskey which he carefully places back in the pantry,
not making a sound, hangs up overcoat, then puts suit-
coat on back of chair. Starts to go upstairs. But* LOLA
speaks)

Doc? That you, Doc?

(*Then* DOC *quietly walks in from kitchen. He is stag-
gering drunk, but he is managing for a few minutes to
appear as though he were perfectly sober and nothing
had happened. His steps, however, are not too sure and
his eyes are like blurred ink pots.* LOLA *is too frightened
to talk. Her mouth is gaping and she is breathless with
fear.*)

DOC

Good morning, honey.

LOLA

Doc! You all right?

DOC

The morning paper here? I wanta see the morning paper.

LOLA

Doc, we don't get a morning paper. *You* know that.

DOC

Oh, then I suppose I'm drunk or something. That what
you're trying to say?

LOLA

No, Doc . . .

DOC

Then give me the morning paper.

LOLA

(*Scampering to get last night's paper from console table*)
Sure, Doc. Here it is. Now you just sit there and be quiet.

DOC

(*Resistance rising*)

Why shouldn't I be quiet?

LOLA

Nothin', Doc . . .

DOC

(*Has trouble unfolding paper. He places it before his face in order not to be seen. But he is too blind even to see*)

Nothing, Doc. (*Mockingly.*)

LOLA

(*Cautiously, after a few minutes' silence*)

Doc, are you all right?

DOC

Of course, I'm all right. Why shouldn't I be all right?

LOLA

Where you been?

DOC

What's it your business where I been? I been to London to see the Queen. What do you think of that? (*Apparently she doesn't know what to think of it*) Just let me alone. That's all I ask. I'm all right.

LOLA

(*Whimpering*)

Doc, what made you do it? You said you'd be home last night . . . 'cause we were having company. Bruce was here and I had a big dinner fixed . . . and you never came. What was the matter, Doc?

DOC

(*Mockingly*)

We had a big dinner for *Bruce*.

LOLA

Doc, it was for you, too.

DOC

Well . . . I don't want it.

LOLA

Don't get mad, Doc.

DOC
(*Threateningly*)

Where's Marie?

LOLA

I don't know, Doc. She didn't come in last night. She was
out with Bruce.

DOC
(*Back to audience*)

I suppose you tucked them in bed together and pecked
through the keyhole and applauded.

LOLA
(*Sickened*)

Doc, don't talk that way. Bruce is a nice boy. They're gonna
get married.

DOC

He probably *has* to marry her, the poor bastard. Just 'cause
she's pretty and he got amorous one day . . . Just like I had
to marry *you*.

LOLA

Oh, Doc!

DOC

You and Marie are both a couple of sluts.

LOLA

Doc, please don't talk like that.

DOC

What are you good for? You can't even get up in the morning and cook my breakfast.

LOLA
(*Mumbling*)
I will, Doc. I will after this.

DOC

You won't even sweep the floors, till some bozo comes along to make love to Marie, and then you fix things up like Buckingham Palace or a Chinese whorehouse with perfume on the lampbulbs, and flowers, and the gold-trimmed china *my mother* gave us. We're not going to use these any more. My mother didn't buy those dishes for whores to eat off of.
(*He jerks the cloth off the table, sending the dishes rattling to the floor.*)

LOLA
Doc! Look what you done.

DOC

Look what I *did,* not *done.* I'm going to get me a drink.
(*Goes to kitchen.*)

LOLA
(*Follows to platform*)
Oh, no, Doc! You know what it does to you!

DOC

You're damn right I know what it does to me. It makes me willing to come home here and look at you, you two-ton old heifer. (*Takes a long swallow*) There! And pretty soon I'm going to have another, then another.

LOLA

(With dread)

Oh, Doc! (LOLA *takes phone.* DOC *sees this, rushes for the butcher-knife from kitchen-cabinet drawer. Not finding it, he gets a hatchet from the back porch)* Mr. Anderson? Come quick, Mr. Anderson. He's back. He's *back!* He's got a hatchet!

DOC

God damn you! Get away from that telephone. (*He chases her into living room where she gets the couch between them*) That's right, phone! Tell the world I'm drunk. Tell the whole damn world. Scream your head off, you fat slut. Holler till all the neighbors think I'm beatin' hell outuv you. Where's Bruce now—under Marie's bed? You got all fresh and pretty for him, didn't you? Combed your hair for once—you even washed the back of your neck and put on a girdle. You were willing to harness all that fat into one bundle.

LOLA

(About to faint under the weight of the crushing accusations)

Doc, don't say any more . . . I'd rather you hit me with an axe, Doc. . . . Honest I would. But I can't stand to hear you talk like that.

DOC

I oughta hack off all that fat, and then wait for Marie and chop off those pretty ankles she's always dancing around on . . . then start lookin' for Turk and fix him too.

LOLA

Daddy, you're talking crazy!

DOC

I'm making sense for the first time in my life. You didn't know I knew about it, did you? But I saw him coming outa there, I saw him. You knew about it all the time and thought you were hidin' something . . .

LOLA

Daddy, I didn't know anything about it at all. Honest, Daddy.

DOC

Then *you're* the one that's crazy, if you think I didn't know. You were running a regular house, weren't you? It's probably been going on for years, ever since we were married.
> (*He lunges for her. She breaks for kitchen. They struggle in front of sink.*)

LOLA

Doc, it's not so; it's not so. You gotta believe me, Doc.

DOC

You're lyin'. But none a that's gonna happen any more. I'm gonna fix you now, once and for all. . . .

LOLA

Doc . . . don't do that to me. (LOLA, *in a frenzy of fear, clutches him around the neck holding arm with axe by his side*) Remember, Doc. It's *me*, Lola! You said I was the prettiest girl you ever saw. Remember, Doc! It's me! Lola!

DOC

(*The memory has overpowered him. He collapses, slowly mumbling*)

Lola . . . my pretty Lola.
> (*He passes out on the floor.* LOLA *stands now, as though in a trance. Quietly* MRS. COFFMAN *comes creeping in through the back way.*)

MRS. COFFMAN
(*Calling softly*)

Mrs. Delaney! (LOLA *doesn't even hear*. MRS. COFFMAN *comes in*) Mrs. Delaney! Here you are, Lady. I heard screaming and I was frightened for you.

LOLA

I . . . I'll be all right . . . some men are comin' pretty soon; everything'll be all right.

MRS. COFFMAN

I'll stay until they get here.

LOLA
(*Feeling a sudden need*)

Would you . . . would you *please*, Mrs. Coffman?
(*Breaks into sobs.*)

MRS. COFFMAN

Of course, Lady. (*Regarding* DOC) The doctor got "sick" again?

LOLA
(*Mumbling*)

Some men . . . 'll be here pretty soon . . .

MRS. COFFMAN

I'll try to straighten things up before they get here. . . . (*She rights chair, hangs up telephone and picks up the axe, which she is holding when* ED ANDERSON *and* ELMO HUSTON *enter unannounced. They are experienced AA's. Neatly dressed businessmen approaching middle-age.*)

ED

Pardon us for walking right in, Mrs. Delaney, but I didn't want to waste a second. (*Kneels by* DOC.)

LOLA
(*Weakly*)

It's all right. . . .
(*Both men observe* DOC *on the floor, and their expressions hold understanding mixed with a feeling of irony. There is even a slight smile of irony on* ED's *face. They have developed the surgeon's objectivity.*)

ED

Where is the hatchet? (*To* ELMO *as though appraising* DOC's *condition*) What do you think, Elmo?

ELMO

We can't leave him here if he's gonna play around with hatchets.

ED

Give me a hand, Elmo. We'll get him to sit up and then try to talk some sense into him. (*They struggle with the lumpy body,* DOC *grunting his resistance*) Come on, Doc, old boy. It's Ed and Elmo. We're going to take care of you. (*They seat him at table.*)

DOC
(*Through a thick fog*)

Lemme alone.

ED

Wake up. We're taking you away from here.

DOC

Lemme 'lone, God damn it.
(*Falls forward, head on table.*)

ELMO
(*To* MRS. COFFMAN)

Is there any coffee?

MRS. COFFMAN

I think so, I'll see.

(*Goes to stove with cup from drainboard. Lights fire under coffee and waits for it to get heated.*)

ED

He's way beyond coffee.

ELMO

It'll help some. Get something hot into his stomach.

ED

If we could get him to eat. How 'bout some hot food, Doc?
(DOC *gestures and they don't push the matter.*)

ELMO

City Hospital, Ed?

ED

I guess that's what it will have to be.

LOLA

Where you going to take him?
(ELMO *goes to phone; speaks quietly to City Hospital.*)

ED

Don't know. Wanta talk to him first.

MRS. COFFMAN

(*Coming in with the coffee*)

Here's the coffee.

ED

(*Taking cup*)

Hold him, Elmo, while I make him swallow this.

ELMO

Come on, Doc, drink your coffee.
(DOC *only blubbers.*)

DOC

(*After the coffee is down*)

Uh . . . what . . . what's goin' on here?

ED

It's me, Doc. Your old friend Ed. I got Elmo with me.

DOC

(*Twisting his face painfully*)

Get out, both of you. Lemme 'lone.

ED

(*With certainty*)

We're takin' you with us, Doc.

DOC

Hell you are. I'm all right. I just had a little slip. We all
have slips. . . .

ED

Sometimes, Doc, but we gotta get over 'em.

DOC

I'll be O.K. Just gimme a day to sober up. I'll be as good as
new.

ED

Remember the last time, Doc? You said you'd be all right
in the morning and we found you with a broken collar bone.
Come on.

DOC

Boys, I'll be all right. Now lemme alone.

ED

How much has he had, Mrs. Delaney?

LOLA

I don't know. He had a quart when he left here yesterday and he didn't get home till now.

ED

He's probably been through a *couple* of quarts. He's been dry for a long time. It's going to hit him pretty hard. Yah, he'll be a pretty sick man for a few days. (*Louder to* DOC, *as though he were talking to a deaf man*) Wanta go to the City Hospital, Doc?

DOC

(*This has a sobering effect on him. He looks about him furtively for possible escape*)

No . . . no, boys. Don't take me there. That's a torture chamber. No, Ed. You wouldn't do that to me.

ED

They'll sober you up.

DOC

Ed, I been there; I've seen the place. That's where they take the crazy people. You can't do that to me, Ed.

ED

Well, *you're* crazy, aren't you? Goin' after your wife with a hatchet.

(*They lift* DOC *to his feet.* DOC *looks with dismal pleading in his eyes at* LOLA, *who has her face in her hands.*)

DOC

(*So plaintive, a sob in his voice*)

Honey! Honey!

(LOLA *can't look at him. Now* DOC *tries to make a getaway, bolting blindly into the living room before the two men catch him and hold him in front of living-room table*)

Honey, don't let 'em take me there. They'll believe *you*. Tell 'em you won't *let* me take a drink.

LOLA

Isn't there any place else you could take him?

ED

Private sanitariums cost a lotta dough.

LOLA

I got forty dollars in the kitchen.

ED

That won't be near enough.

DOC

I'll be at the meeting tomorrow night sober as you are now.

ED
(To LOLA)

All the king's horses couldn't keep him from takin' another drink now, Mrs. Delaney. He got himself into this; he's gotta sweat it out.

DOC

I won't go to the City Hospital. That's where they take the crazy people.
(Stumbles into chair.)

ED
(Using all his patience now)

Look, Doc. Elmo and I are your friends. You know that. Now if you don't come along peacefully, we're going to call the cops and you'll have to wear off this jag in the cooler.

How'd you like that? (DOC *is as though stunned*) The important thing is for you to get sober.

DOC

I don't wanta go.

ED

The City Hospital or the City Jail. Take your choice. We're not going to leave you here. Come on, Elmo.
(*They grab hold of him.*)

DOC

(*Has collected himself and now given in*)
O.K., boys. Gimme another drink and I'll go.

LOLA

Oh, no, Doc.

ED

Might as well humor him, ma'am. Another few drinks couldn't make much difference now.
(MRS. COFFMAN *runs for bottle and glass in pantry and comes right back with them. She hands them to* LOLA.)
O.K., Doc, we're goin' to give you a drink. Take a good one; it's gonna be your last for a long, long time to come.
(ED *takes the bottle, removes the cork and gives* DOC *a glass of whiskey.* DOC *takes his fill, straight, coming up once or twice for air. Then* ED *takes the bottle from him and hands it to* LOLA. *To* LOLA)
They'll keep him three or four days, Mrs. Delaney; then he'll be home again, good as new. (*Modestly*) I . . . I don't want to pry into personal affairs, ma'am . . . but he'll need you then, pretty bad . . . Come on, Doc. Let's go.

(ED *has a hold of* DOC's *coat sleeve trying to maneuver him. A faraway look is in* DOC's *eyes, a dazed look containing panic and fear. He gets to his feet.*)

DOC
(*Struggling to sound reasonable*)
Just a minute, boys . . .

ED
What's the matter?

DOC
I . . . I wanta glass of water.

ED
You'll get a glass of water later. Come on.

DOC
(*Beginning to twist a little in* ED's *grasp*)
. . . a glass of water . . . that's all . . .
(*One furious, quick twist of his body and he eludes* ED.)

ED
Quick, Elmo.
(ELMO *acts fast and they get* DOC *before he gets away. Then* DOC *struggles with all his might, kicking and screaming like a pampered child,* ED *and* ELMO *holding him tightly to usher him out.*)

DOC
(*As he is led out*)
Don't let 'em take me there. Don't take me there. Stop them, somebody. Stop them. That's where they take the crazy people. Oh, God, stop them, somebody. Stop them.
(LOLA *looks on blankly while* ED *and* ELMO *depart with* DOC. *Now there are several moments of deep silence.*)

MRS. COFFMAN
(*Clears up. Very softly*)
Is there anything more I can do for you now, Mrs. Delaney?

LOLA
I guess not.

MRS. COFFMAN
(*Puts a hand on* LOLA's *shoulder*)
Get busy, Lady. Get busy and forget it.

LOLA
Yes . . . I'll get busy right away. Thanks, Mrs. Coffman.

MRS. COFFMAN
I better go. I've got to make breakfast for the children. If you want me for anything, let me know.

LOLA
Yes . . . yes . . . good-bye, Mrs. Coffman.
(MRS. COFFMAN *exits.* LOLA *is too exhausted to move from the big chair. At first she can't even cry; then the tears come slowly, softly. In a few moments* BRUCE *and* MARIE *enter, bright and merry.* LOLA *turns her head slightly to regard them as creatures from another planet.*)

MARIE
(*Springing into room.* BRUCE *follows*)
Congratulate me, Mrs. Delaney.

LOLA
Huh?

MARIE
We're going to be married.

LOLA

Married? (*It barely registers.*)

MARIE

(*Showing ring*)

Here it is. My engagement ring.

(MARIE *and* BRUCE *are too engrossed in their own happiness to notice* LOLA's *stupor.*)

LOLA

That's lovely . . . lovely.

MARIE

We've had the most wonderful time. We danced all night and then drove out to the lake and saw the sun rise.

LOLA

That's nice.

MARIE

We've made all our plans. I'm quitting school and flying back to Cincinnati with Bruce this afternoon. His mother has invited me to visit them before I go home. Isn't that wonderful?

LOLA

Yes . . . yes, indeed.

MARIE

Going to miss me?

LOLA

Yes, of course, Marie. We'll miss you very much . . . uh . . . congratulations.

MARIE

Thanks, Mrs Delaney. (*Goes to bedroom door*) Come on, Bruce, help me get my stuff. (*To* LOLA) Mrs. Delaney, would you throw everything into a big box and send it to me at home? We haven't had breakfast yet. We're going down to the hotel and celebrate.

BRUCE

I'm sorry we're in such a hurry, but we've got a taxi waiting.
(*They go into room.*)

LOLA

(*Goes to telephone, dials*)
Long-distance? I want to talk to Green Valley 223. Yes This is Delmar 1887.
(*She hangs up.* MARIE *comes from bedroom, followed by* BRUCE, *who carries suitcase.*)

MARIE

Mrs. Delaney, I sure hate to say good-bye to you. You've been so wonderful to me. But Bruce says I can come and visit you once in a while, didn't you, Bruce?

BRUCE

Sure thing.

LOLA

You're going?

MARIE

We're going downtown and have our breakfast, then do a little shopping and catch our plane. And thanks for everything, Mrs. Delaney.

BRUCE

It was very nice of you to have us to dinner.

LOLA

Dinner? Oh, don't mention it.

MARIE
(*To* LOLA)

There isn't much time for good-bye now, but I just want you to know Bruce and I wish you the best of everything. You and Doc both. Tell Doc good-bye for me, will you, and remember I think you're both a coupla peaches.

BRUCE

Hurry, honey.

MARIE

'Bye, Mrs. Delaney! (*She goes out.*)

BRUCE

'Bye, Mrs. Delaney. Thanks for being nice to my girl.
(*He goes out and off porch with* MARIE.)

LOLA

(*Waves. The phone rings. She goes to it quickly*)

Hello. Hello, Mom. It's Lola, Mom. How are you? Mom, Doc's sick again. Do you think Dad would let me come home for a while? I'm awfully unhappy, Mom. Do you think . . . just till I made up my mind? . . . All right. No, I guess it wouldn't do any good for you to come here . . . I . . . I'll let you know what I decide to do. That's all, Mom. Thanks. Tell Daddy hello.

(*She hangs up.*)

Curtain

Scene IV

It is morning, a week later. The house is neat again. LOLA *is dusting in the living room as* MRS. COFFMAN *enters.*

MRS. COFFMAN

Mrs. Delaney! Good morning, Mrs. Delaney.

LOLA

Come in, Mrs. Coffman.

MRS. COFFMAN
(*Coming in*)

It's a fine day for the games. I've got a box lunch ready, and I'm taking all the kids to the Stadium. My boy's got a ticket for you, too. You better get dressed and come with us.

LOLA

Thanks, Mrs. Coffman, but I've got work to do.

MRS. COFFMAN

But it's a big day. The Spring Relays . . . All the athletes from the colleges are supposed to be there.

LOLA

Oh, yes. You know that boy, Turk, who used to come here to see Marie—he's one of the big stars.

MRS. COFFMAN

Is that so? Come on . . . do. We've got a ticket for you. . . .

LOLA

Oh, no, I have to stay here and clean up the house. Doc may be coming home today. I talked to him on the phone. He wasn't sure what time they'd let him out, but I wanta have the place all nice for him.

MRS. COFFMAN

Well, I'll tell you all about it when I come home. Everybody and his brother will be there.

LOLA

Have a good time.

MRS. COFFMAN

'Bye, Mrs. Delaney.

LOLA

'Bye.

(MRS. COFFMAN *leaves, and* LOLA *goes into kitchen. The* MAILMAN *comes onto porch and leaves a letter, but* LOLA *doesn't even know he's there. Then the* MILKMAN *knocks on the kitchen door.*)

LOLA

Come in.

MILKMAN

(*Entering with armful of bottles, etc.*)
I see you checked the list, lady. You've got a lot of extras.

LOLA

Ya— I think my husband's coming home.

MILKMAN

(*He puts the supplies on table, then pulls out magazine*)
Remember, I told you my picture was going to appear in

Strength and Health. (*Showing her magazine*) Well, see that pile of muscles? That's me.

LOLA

My goodness. You got your picture in a magazine.

MILKMAN

Yes, ma'am. See what it says about my chest development? For the greatest self-improvement in a three months' period.

LOLA

Goodness sakes. You'll be famous, won't you?

MILKMAN

If I keep busy on these bar-bells. I'm working now for "muscular separation."

LOLA

That's nice.

MILKMAN
(*Cheerily*)

Well, good day, ma'am.

LOLA

You forgot your magazine.

MILKMAN

That's for you.
(*Frits* LOLA *puts away the supplies in the icebox. Then* DOC *comes in the front door, carrying the little suitcase she previously packed for him. His quiet manner and his serious demeanor are the same as before.* LOLA *is shocked by his sudden appearance. She jumps and can't help showing her fright.*)

LOLA

Docky!
> (*Without thinking she assumes an attitude of fear.* DOC *observes this and it obviously pains him.*)

DOC

Good morning, honey.
> (*Pause.*)

LOLA
> (*On platform*)

Are . . . are you all right, Doc?

DOC

Yes, I'm all right. (*An awkward pause. Then* DOC *tries to reassure her*) Honest, I'm all right, honey. Please don't stand there like that . . . like I was gonna . . . gonna . . .

LOLA
> (*Tries to relax*)

I'm sorry, Doc.

DOC

How you been?

LOLA

Oh, I been all right, Doc. Fine.

DOC

Any news?

LOLA

I told you about Marie—over the phone.

DOC

Yah.

COME BACK, LITTLE SHEBA

LOLA

He was a very nice boy, Doc. Very nice.

DOC

That's good. I hope they'll be happy.

LOLA

(*Trying to sound bright*)

She said . . . maybe she'd come back and visit us some
time. That's what she *said*.

DOC

(*Pause*)

It . . . it's good to be home.

LOLA

Is it, Daddy?

DOC

Yah.

(*Beginning to choke up, just a little.*)

LOLA

Did everything go all right . . . I mean . . . did they treat
you well and . . .

DOC

(*Now loses control of his feelings. Tears in his eyes, he
all but lunges at her, gripping her arms, drilling his
head into her bosom*)

Honey, don't ever leave me. *Please* don't ever leave me.
If you do, they'd have to keep me down at that place all the
time. I don't know what I said to you or what I did, I can't
remember hardly anything. But please forgive me . . . please
. . . please . . . And I'll try to make everything up.

LOLA

(*There is surprise on her face and new contentment. She becomes almost angelic in demeanor. Tenderly she places a soft hand on his head*)

Daddy! Why, of course I'll never leave you. (*A smile of satisfaction*) You're all I've got. You're all I ever had. (*Very tenderly he kisses her.*)

DOC

(*Collecting himself now.* LOLA *sits beside* DOC)

I . . . I feel better . . . already.

LOLA

(*Almost gay*)

So do I. Have you had your breakfast?

DOC

No. The food there was terrible. When they told me I could go this morning, I decided to wait and fix myself breakfast here.

LOLA

(*Happily*)

Come on out in the kitchen and I'll get you a nice, big breakfast. I'll scramble some eggs and . . . You see I've got the place all cleaned up just the way you like it. (DOC *goes to kitchen*) Now you sit down here and I'll get your fruit juice. (*He sits and she gets fruit juice from refrigerator*) I've got bacon this morning, too. My, it's expensive now. And I'll light the oven and make you some toast, and here's some orange marmalade, and . . .

DOC

(*With a new feeling of control*)

Fruit juice. I'll need lots of fruit juice for a while. The doctor said it would restore the vitamins. You see, that damn whiskey kills all the vitamins in your system, eats up all the sugar in your kidneys. They came around every morning and shot vitamins in my arm. Oh, it didn't hurt. And the doctor told me to drink a quart of fruit juice every day. And you better get some candy bars for me at the grocery this morning. Doctor said to eat lots of candy, try to replace the sugar.

LOLA

I'll do that, Doc. Here's another glass of this pineapple juice now. I'll get some candy bars first thing.

DOC

The doctor said I should have a hobby. Said I should go out more. That's all that's wrong with me. I thought maybe I'd go hunting once in a while.

LOLA

Yes, Doc. And bring home lots of good things to eat.

DOC

I'll get a big bird dog, too. Would you like a sad-looking old bird dog around the house?

LOLA .

Of course, I would. (*All her life and energy have been restored*) You know what, Doc? I had another dream last night.

DOC

About Little Sheba?

LOLA

Oh, it was about everyone and everything. (*In a raptured tone. She gets bacon from icebox and starts to cook it*) Marie and I were going to the Olympics back in our old high school stadium. There were thousands of people there. There was Turk out in the center of the field throwing the javelin. Every time he threw it, the crowd would roar . . . and you know who the man in charge was? It was my father. Isn't that funny? . . . But Turk kept changing into someone else all the time. And then my father disqualified him. So he had to sit on the sidelines . . . and guess who took his place, Daddy? You! You came trotting out there on the field just as big as you please . . .

DOC
(Smilingly)

How did I do, Baby?

LOLA

Fine. You picked the javelin up real careful, like it was awful heavy. But you threw it, Daddy, clear, *clear* up into the sky. And it never came down again. (DOC *looks very pleased with himself.* LOLA *goes on*) Then it started to rain. And I couldn't find Little Sheba. I almost went crazy looking for her and there were so many people, I didn't even know where to look. And you were waiting to take me home. And we walked and walked through the slush and mud, and people were hurrying all around us and . . . and . . . (*Leaves stove and sits. Sentimental tears come to her eyes*) But this part is sad, Daddy. All of a sudden I saw Little Sheba . . . she was lying in the middle of the field . . . dead. . . . It made me cry, Doc. No one paid any attention . . . I cried and cried. It made me feel so bad, Doc. That sweet little puppy . . . her curly white fur all smeared with mud, and no one to stop and take care of her . . .

DOC

Why couldn't *you?*

LOLA

I wanted to, but you wouldn't let me. You kept saying, "We can't stay here, honey; we gotta go on. We gotta go on." (*Pause*) Now, isn't that strange?

DOC

Dreams are funny.

LOLA

I don't think Little Sheba's ever coming back, Doc. I'm not going to call her any more.

DOC

Not much point in it, Baby. I guess she's gone for good.

LOLA

I'll fix your eggs.
> (*She gets up, embraces* DOC, *and goes to stove.* DOC *remains at table sipping his fruit juice. The curtain comes slowly down.*)